C. L. HANON

The Virtuoso Pianist

In Sixty Exercises

For the Piano

For the Acquirement of Agility, Independence,
Strength, and Perfect Evenness in the Fingers,
as well as Suppleness of the Wrist

Translated from the French by
DR. THEODORE BAKER

Book I (Nos. 1-20) — Library Vol. 1071
Book II (Nos. 21-43) — Library Vol. 1072
Book III (Nos. 44-60) — Library Vol. 1073
→ Complete — Library Vol. 925

ECHO POINT BOOKS & MEDIA, LLC

Published 2016 by Echo Point Books & Media
Brattleboro, Vermont
www.EchoPointBooks.com

ISBN: 978-1-62654-590-8 (paperback) / 978-1-62654-591-5 (casebound) / 978-1-62654-592-2 (spiralbound)

Cover design by Justine McFarland

PREFACE.

The study of the piano is now-a-days so general, and good pianists are so numerous, that mediocrity on this instrument is no longer endured. In consequence, one must study the piano eight or ten years before venturing to perform a piece of any difficulty, even at a gathering of amateurs. Now, how few persons are in a position to devote so many years to this study! It often happens, therefore, that for want of sufficient practice the playing is uneven and incorrect. The left hand gives out in passages of slight difficulty; the fourth and fifth fingers are almost useless for lack of special exercises for these fingers, which are always weaker than the rest; and when passages in octaves, in tremolo or trills occur, they are usually executed only by dint of exertion and fatigue, so that the performance is very incorrect and wholly wanting in expression.

For several years we have labored to overcome this state of affairs, making it our aim to unite in one work special exercises which render possible a complete course of pianistic study in far less time.

To attain this end, it sufficed to find the solution of the following problem:

If all five fingers of the hand were absolutely equally well trained, they would be ready to execute anything written for the instrument, and the only question remaining would be that of fingering, which could be readily solved.

We have found the solution of this problem in our work "The Virtuoso-Pianist, in 60 Exercises," etc. In this volume will be found the exercises necessary for the acquirement of agility, independence, strength and perfect evenness in the fingers, as well as suppleness of the wrists—all indispensable qualities for fine execution; furthermore, these exercises are calculated to render the left hand equally skilful with the right. Excepting a few exercises, to be found in several methods, the entire book is our personal work. These exercises are interesting, and do not fatigue the student like the generality of five-finger exercises, which are so dry that one requires the perseverance of a true artist to summon up courage to study them.

These exercises are written in such a manner that, after having read them a few times, they can be played in quite a rapid movement; they thus become

PREFACE.—*Continued.*

excellent practice for the fingers, and one loses no time in studying them. If desired, any of these exercises may be played on several pianos simultaneously, rousing a spirit of emulation among the students, and habituating them to ensemble-playing.

All descriptions of difficulties will be met with. The exercises are so arranged, that in each successive number the fingers are rested from the fatigue caused by the one preceding. The result of this combination is, that all mechanical difficulties are executed without effort or weariness; and, after such practice, the fingers attain to astonishing facility of execution.

This work is intended for all piano-pupils. It may be taken up after the pupil has studied about a year. As for more advanced students, they will study it in a very short time, and will thereafter never experience the stiffness which may have been previously felt in fingers or wrists; this will render them capable of surmounting the principal mechanical difficulties.

Pianists and teachers who cannot find time for sufficient practice to keep up their playing, need only to play these exercises a few hours in order to regain all the dexterity of their fingers.

This entire volume can be played through in an hour; and if, after it has been thoroughly mastered, it be repeated daily for a time, difficulties will disappear as if by enchantment, and that beautiful, clear, clean, pearling execution will have been acquired which is the secret of distinguished artists.

Finally, we offer this work as giving the key to all mechanical difficulties. We therefore consider that we are rendering a real service to young pianists, to teachers, and to the directors of boarding-schools, in proposing their adoption of our work, "The Virtuoso-Pianist."

The Virtuoso-Pianist.

Part I.

Preparatory Exercises for the Acquirement of Agility, Independence, Strength and Perfect Evenness in the Fingers.

Nº 1.

Stretch between the fifth and fourth fingers of the left hand in ascending, and the fifth and fourth fingers of the right hand in descending.

For studying the 20 exercises in this First Part, begin with the metronome set at 60, gradually increasing the speed up to 108; this is the meaning of the double metronome-mark at the head of each exercise.

Lift the fingers high and with precision, playing each note very distinctly.

C. L. HANON.

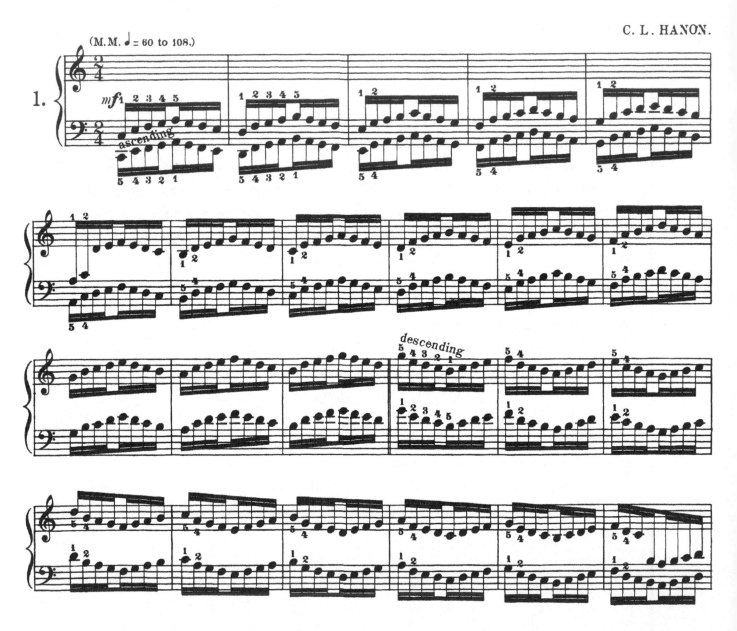

(1) For brevity, we shall henceforward indicate only by their figures those fingers which are to be specially trained in each exercise; e. g., 3-4 in Nº 2; 2-3-4 in Nº 3, etc.

Observe that, throughout the book, both hands are continually executing the same difficulties; in this way the left hand becomes as skilful as the right. Besides, the difficulties executed by the left hand in ascending, are exactly copied by the same fingers of the right hand in descending; this new style of exercise will cause the hands to acquire perfect equality.

As soon as Ex. 1 is mastered, go on to Ex. 2 without stopping on this note.

№ 2.

(3-4) When this exercise is mastered, recommence the preceding one, and play both together four times without interruption; the fingers will gain considerably by practising these exercises, and those following, in this way.

(1) The fourth and fifth fingers being naturally weak, it should be observed that this exercise, and those following it up to № 31, are intended to render them as strong and agile as the second and third.

No 3.

(2-3-4) Before beginning to practise No 3, play through the preceding exercises once or twice without stopping. When No 3 is mastered, practise No 4, and then No 5, and as soon as they are thoroughly learned play through all three at least four times without interruption, not stopping until the last note on page 6. The entire work should be practised in this manner. Therefore, when playing the numbers in the First Part, stop only on the last note on pp. 3, 6, 9, 12, 15, 18, and 21.

(3-4-5) (1) Special exercise for the **3rd**, **4th** and **5th** fingers of the hand.

Nº 5.

(1-2-3-4-5) We repeat, that the fingers should be lifted high, and with precision, until this entire volume is mastered.

(1) Preparation for the trill with the 4th and 5th fingers of the right hand.

(5) To obtain the good results which we promise those who study this work, it is indispensable to play daily, at least once, the exercises already learned.

Nᵒ 7.

(3-4-5) Exercise of the greatest importance for the 3rd, 4th and 5th fingers.

№ 8.

(1-2-3-4-5) Very important exercise for all five fingers.

№ 9.

Extension of the 4<u>th</u> and 5<u>th</u>, and general finger-exercise.

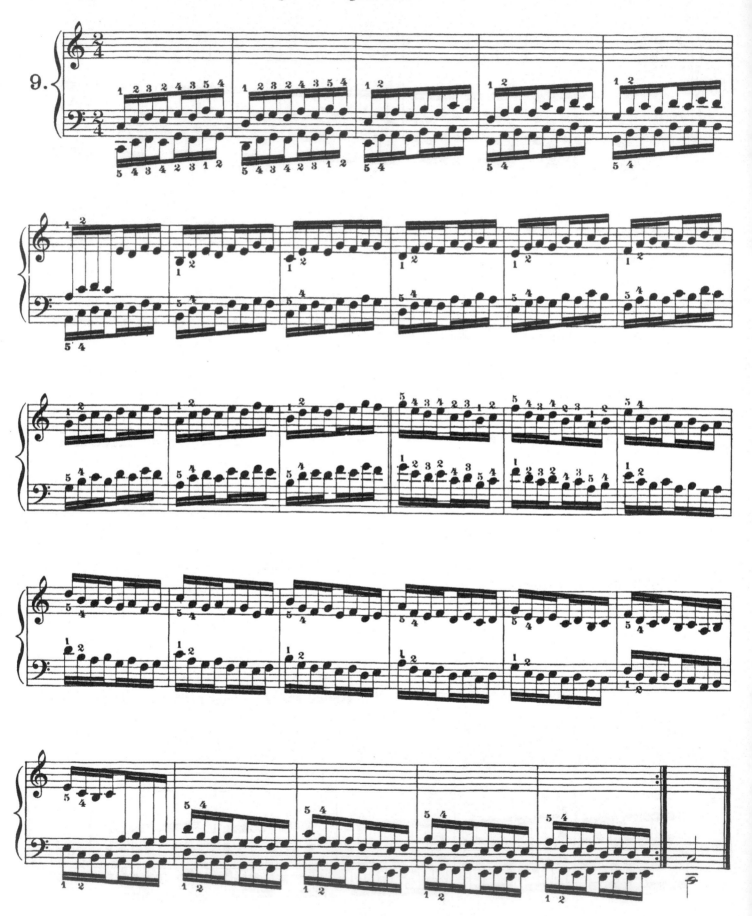

(3-4) Preparation for the trill, for the 3rd and 4th fingers of the left hand in ascending (1); and for the 3rd and 4th of the right, descending (2).

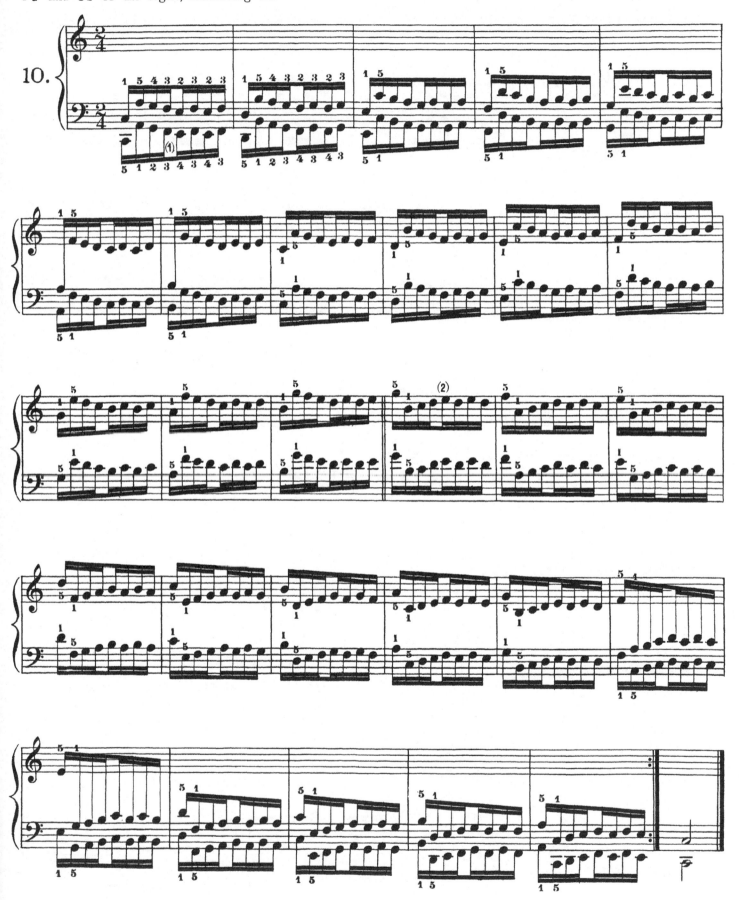

№ 11.

(3-4-5) Another preparation for the trill, for the 4th and 5th fingers.

Extension of 1-5, and exercise for 3-4-5.

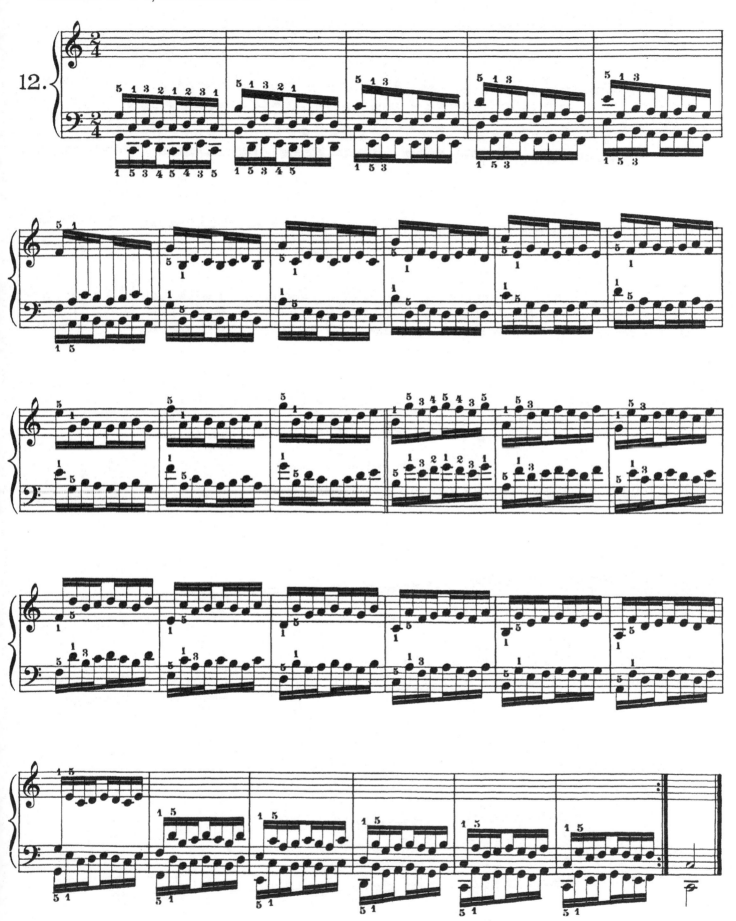

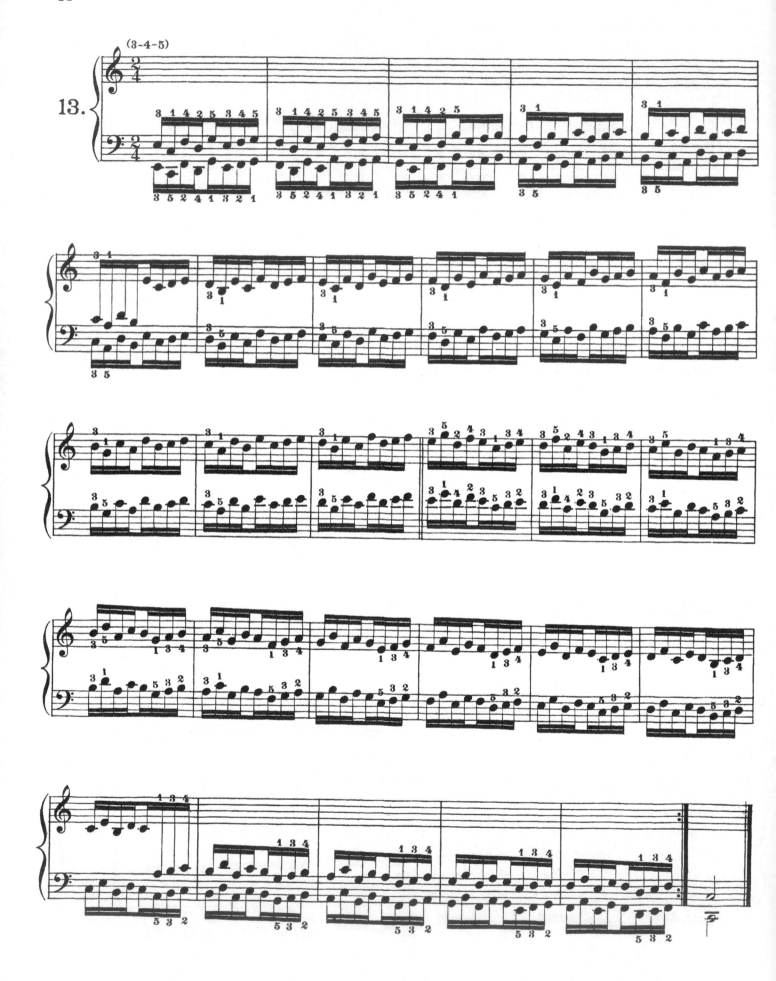

(3-4) Another preparation for the trill, for the 3rd and 4th fingers.

14.

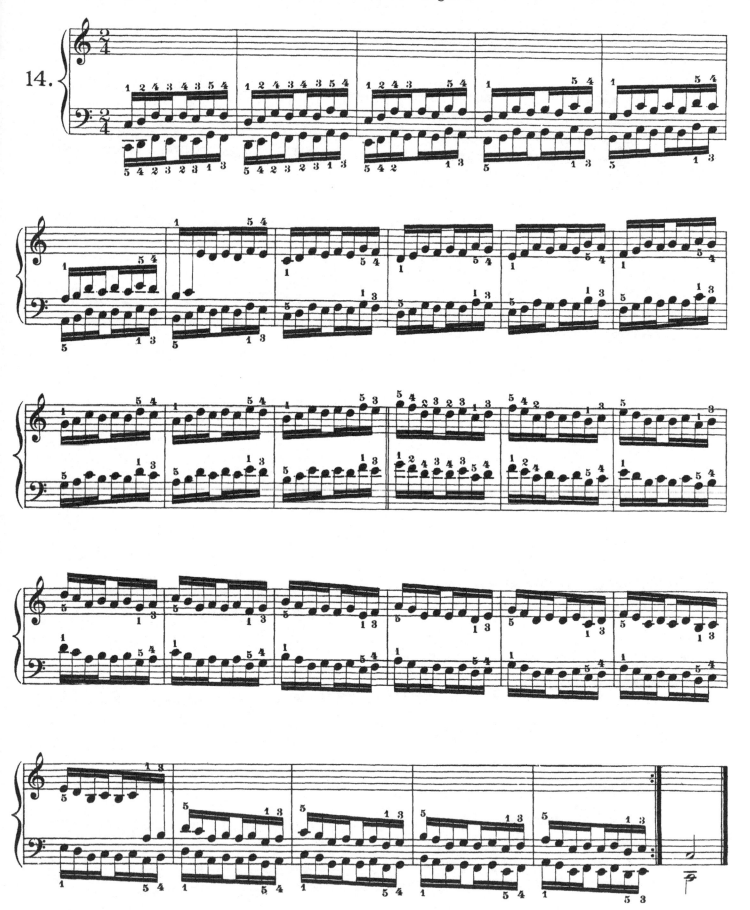

16

Extension of 1-2, and exercise for all **5** fingers.

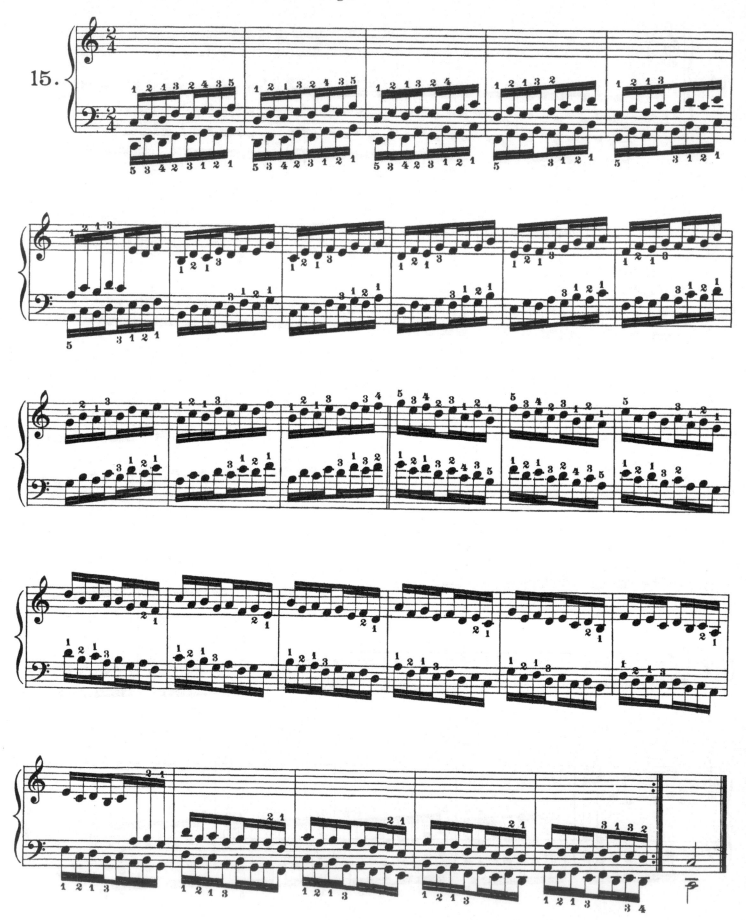

Extension of **3-5**, and exercise for **3-4-5**.

18

Extension of 1-2, 2-4, 4-5, and exercise for 3-4-5.

17.

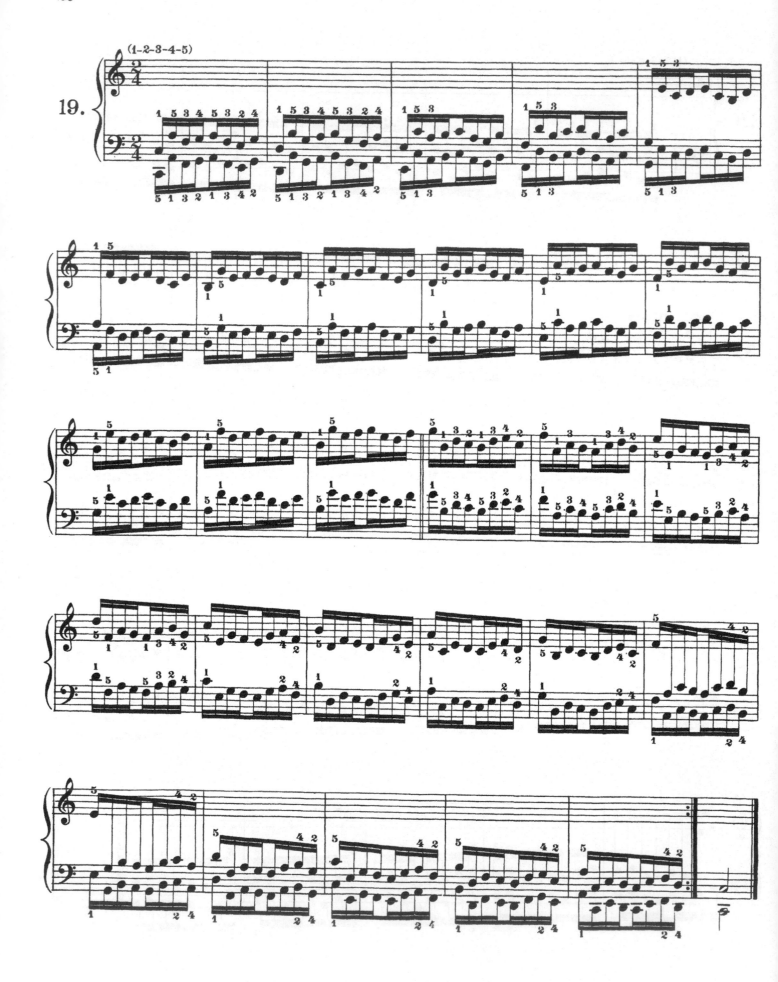

Extension of 2-4, 4-5, and exercise for 2-3-4.

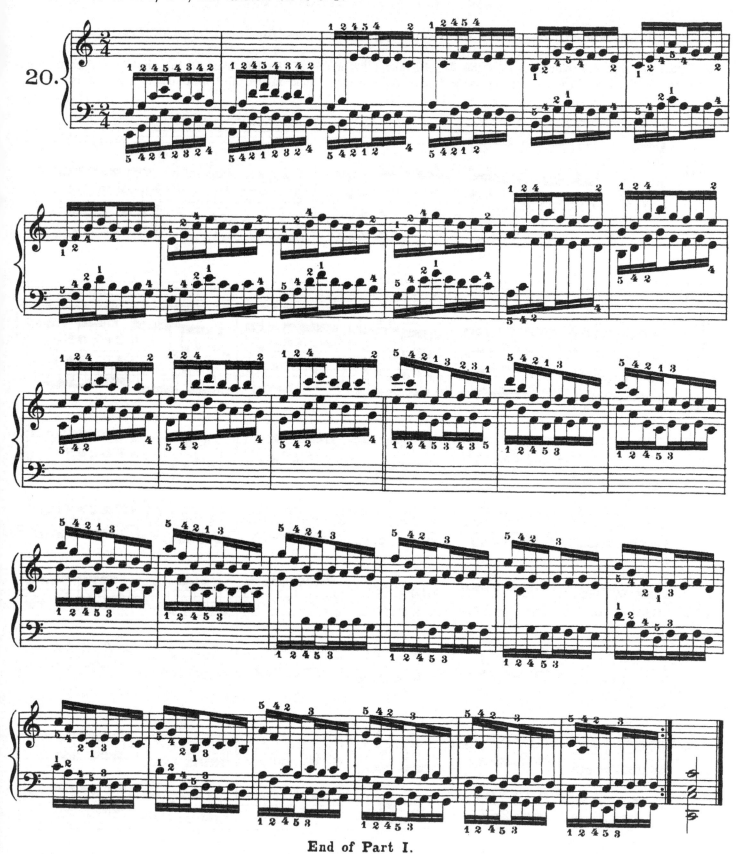

End of Part I.

After having mastered this First Part, play it through once or twice daily for some time before commencing the study of the Second ("transcendent") Part; by so doing, one is sure to obtain every possible advantage that this work promises. Complete mastery of Part I gives the key to the difficulties found in Part II.

The Virtuoso-Pianist. Part II

Transcendent Exercises for Preparing the Fingers for the Virtuoso Exercises.

Observe, that the work done by the 3rd, 4th and 5th fingers of the left hand in the first beat of each measure (A) is repeated inversely by the same fingers of the right hand in the third beat of the same measure (B).

C. L. HANON

Practise the exercises in Part II, like those in Part I, with the metronome at 60; similarly practise all the following exercises where the tempo is not indicated, and gradually increase the speed to 108. Wherever a different tempo is required, it will be indicated at the head of the exercise.

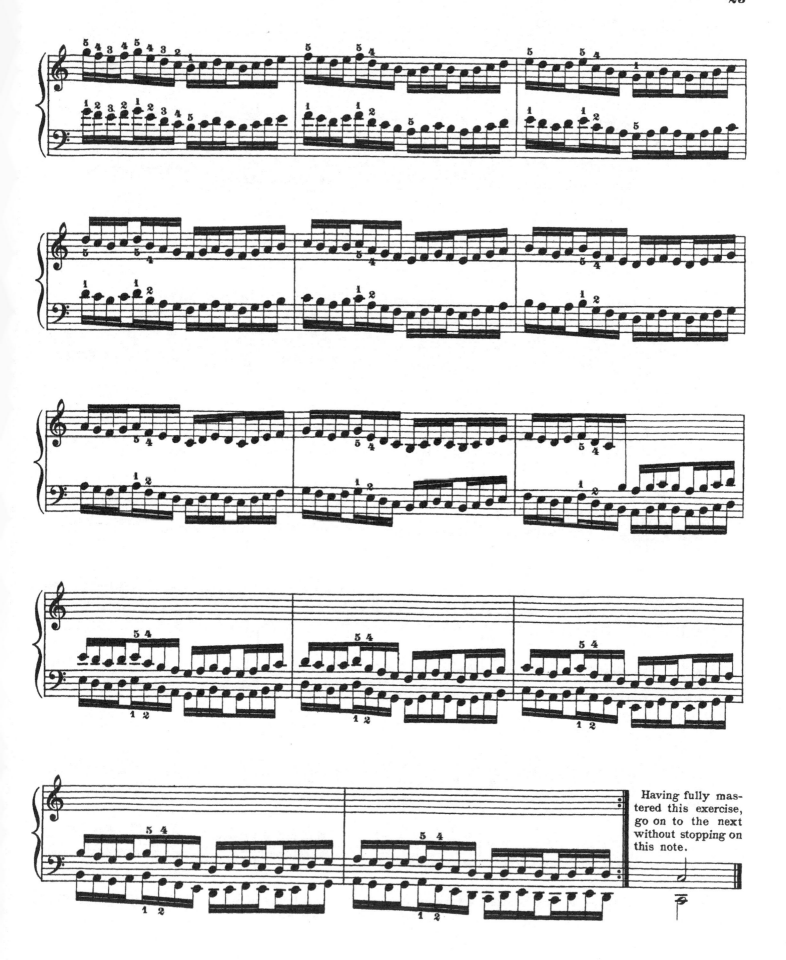

Having fully mas-
tered this exercise,
go on to the next
without stopping on
this note.

Same object as N⁰ 21. (3-4-5)

Practise the exercises of this Second Part as we directed for Part I (top of p. 4); thus, in playing through the exercises, stop only on the last notes on pp. 24, 29, 33, 37, 41, 44, 46, and 49.

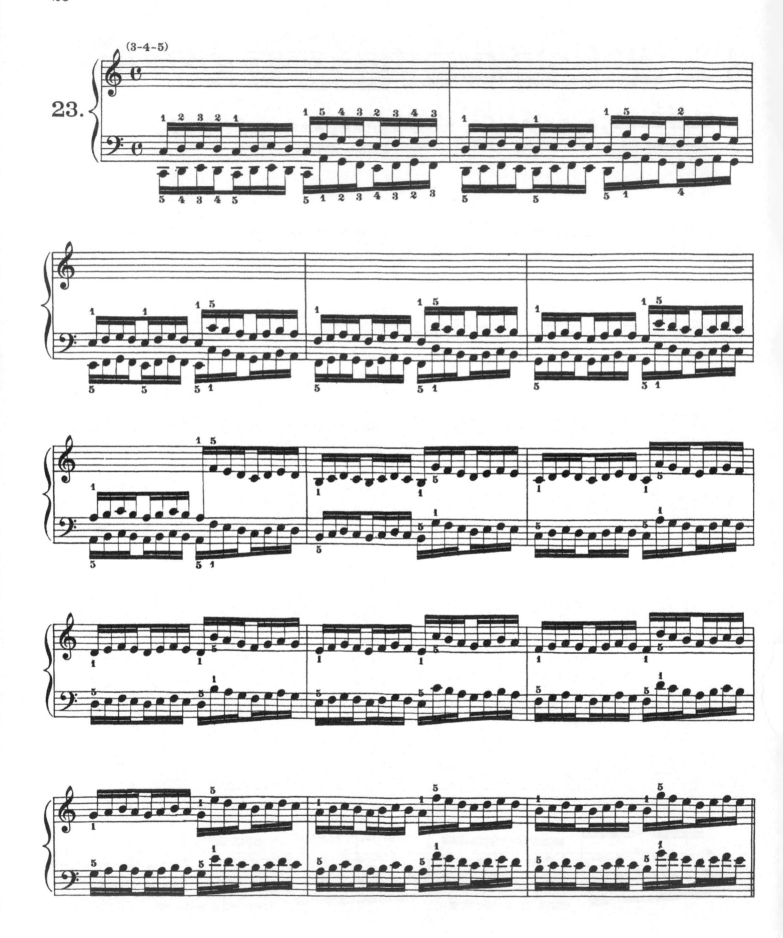

28

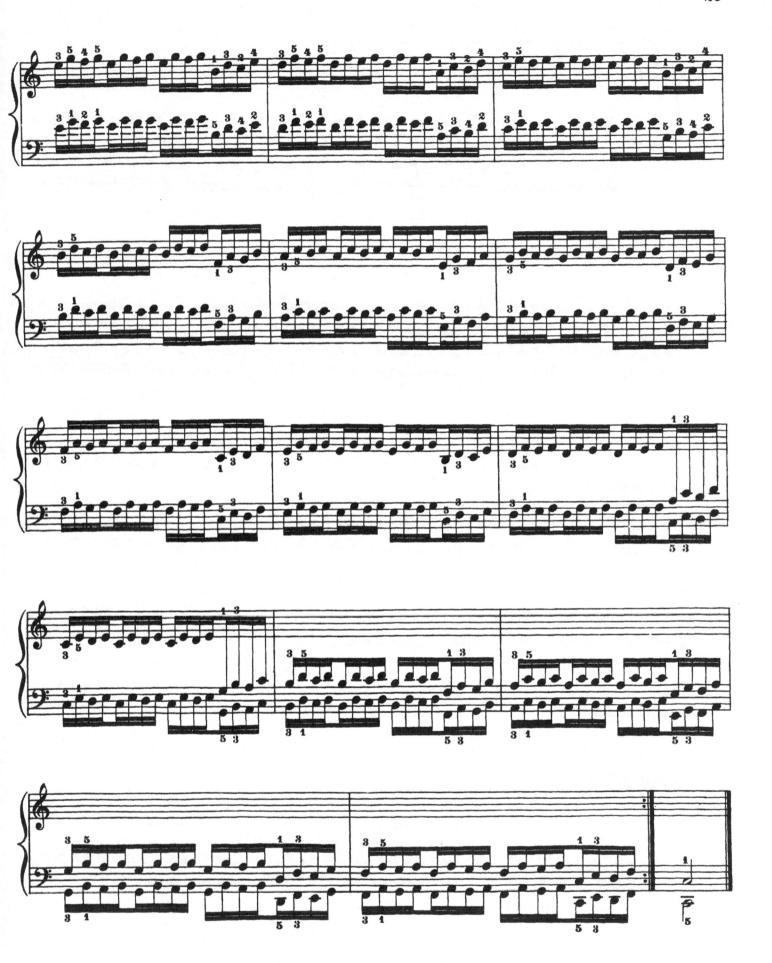

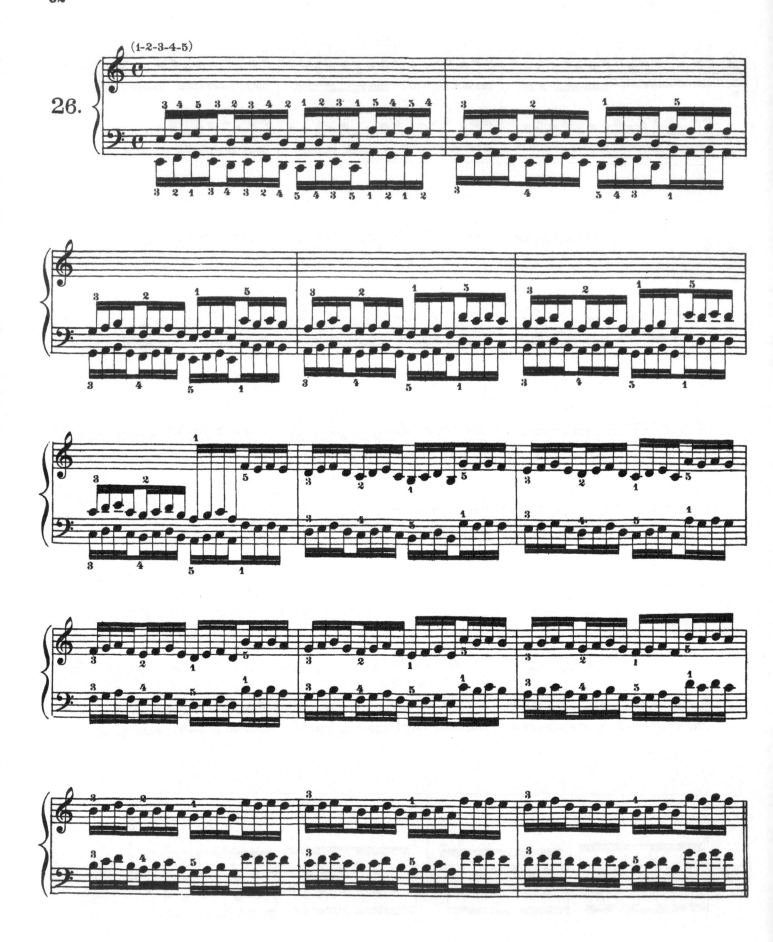

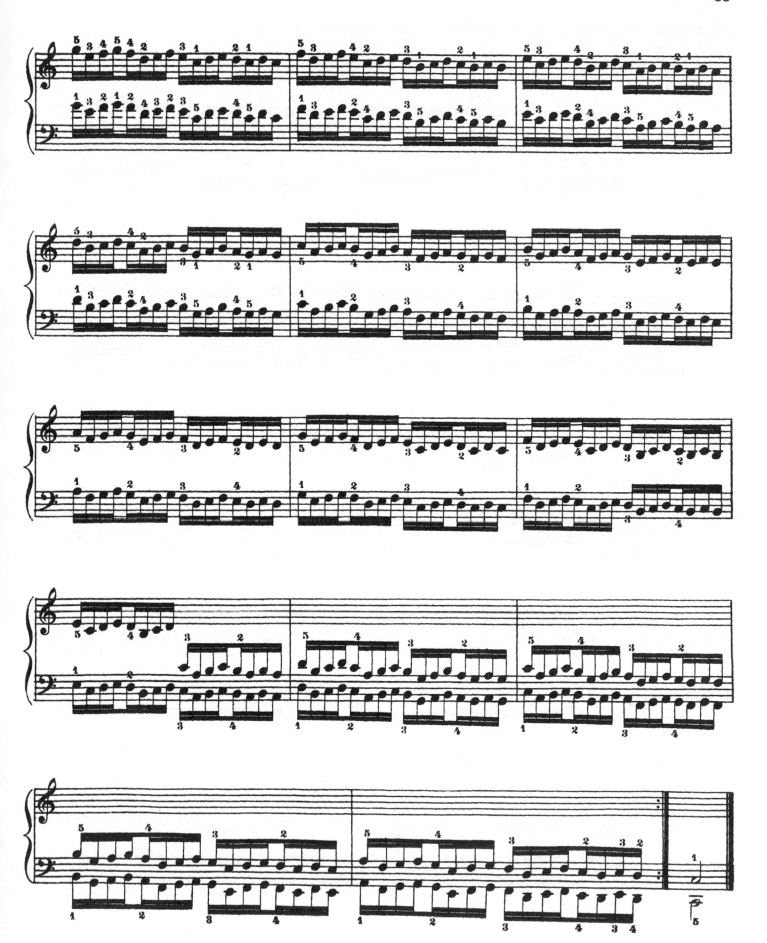

(1-2-3-4-5): Prepares the 4th and 5th fingers for the trill given further on.

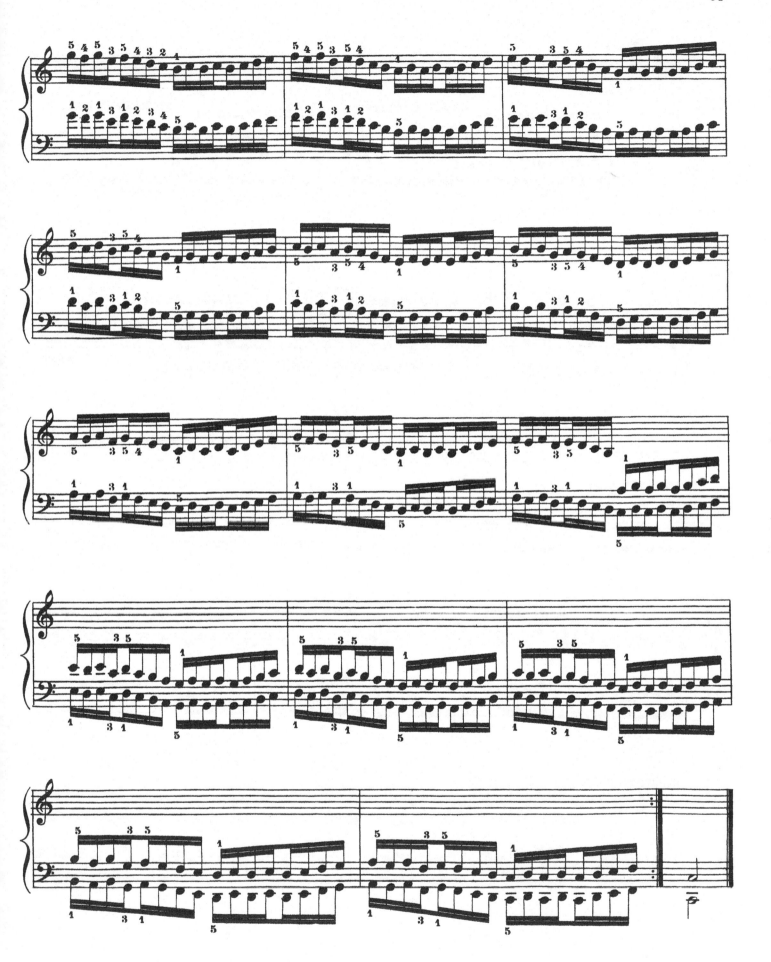

38

(1-2-3-4-5) Preparation for the Trill, for all five fingers.

40

Trill alternating between 1-2 and 4-5.

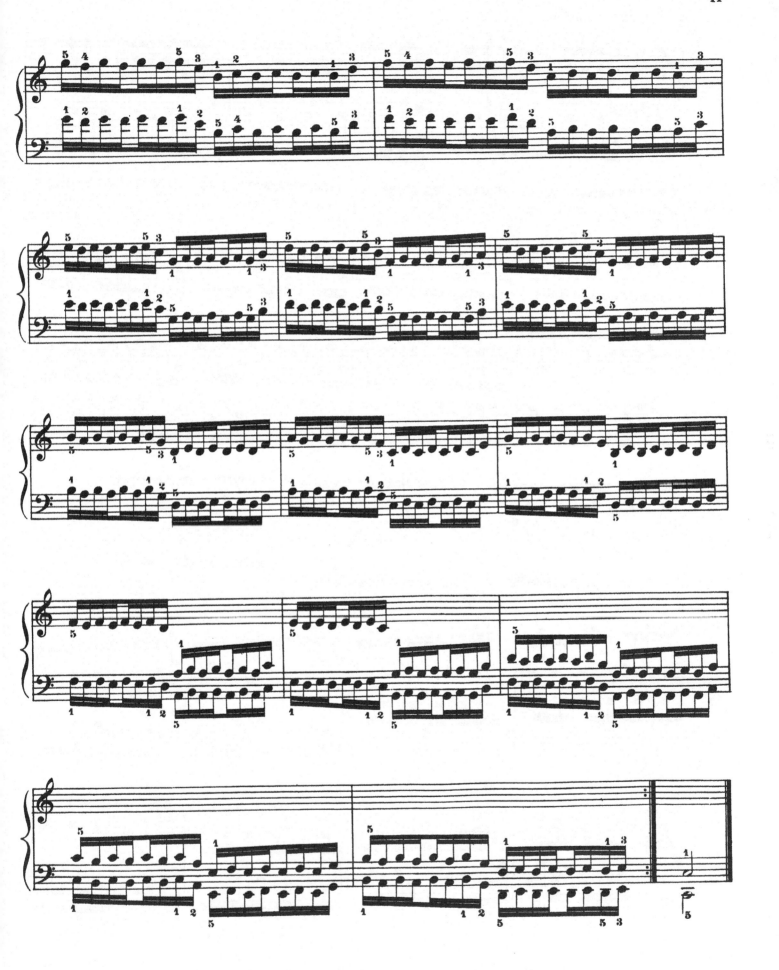

(1-2-3-4-5, and extensions)

31.

Turning the thumb under.

Turning the thumb under the 2nd finger.

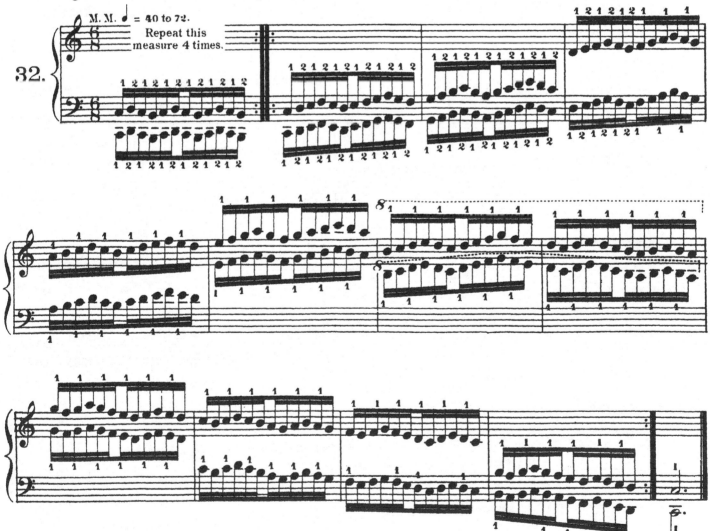

Turning the thumb under the 3rd finger.

33.

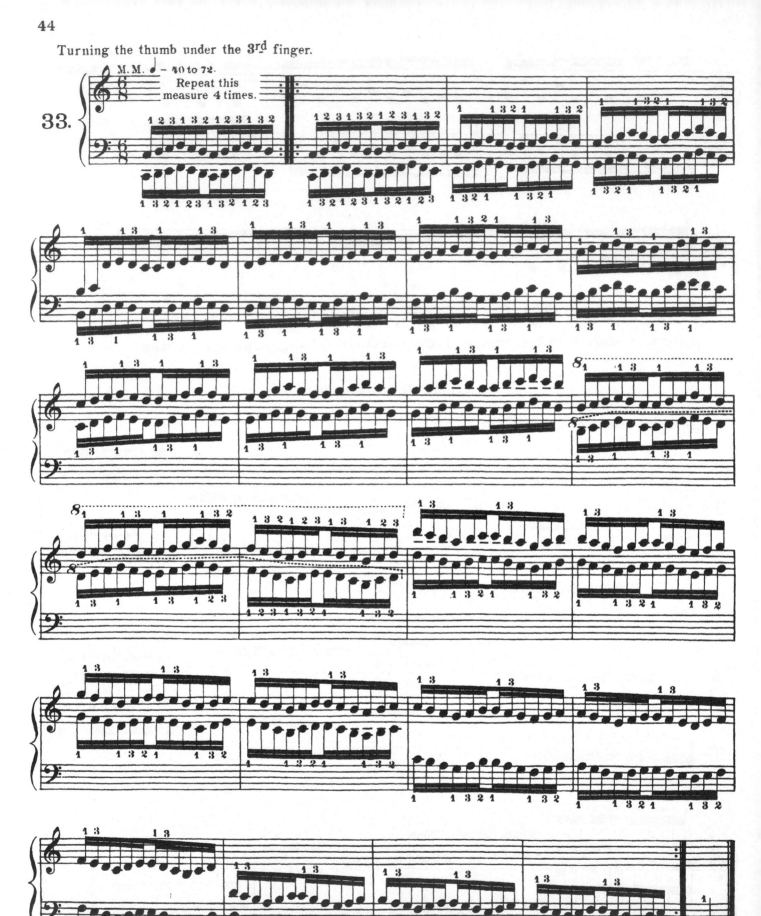

Turning the thumb under the **4**th finger.

34.

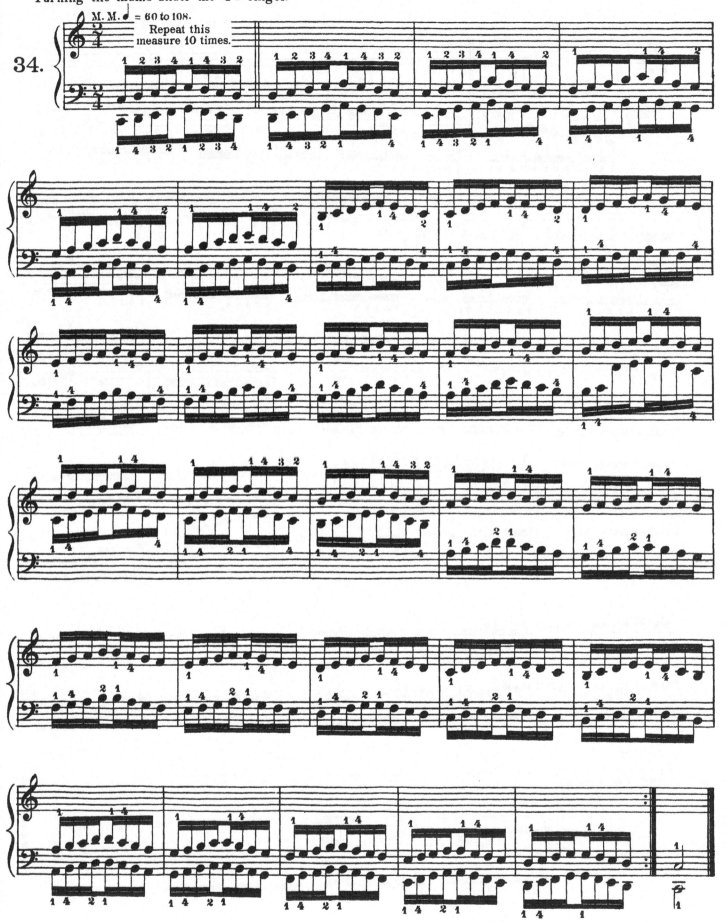

Turning the thumb under the 5th finger. This exercise is of the highest importance.

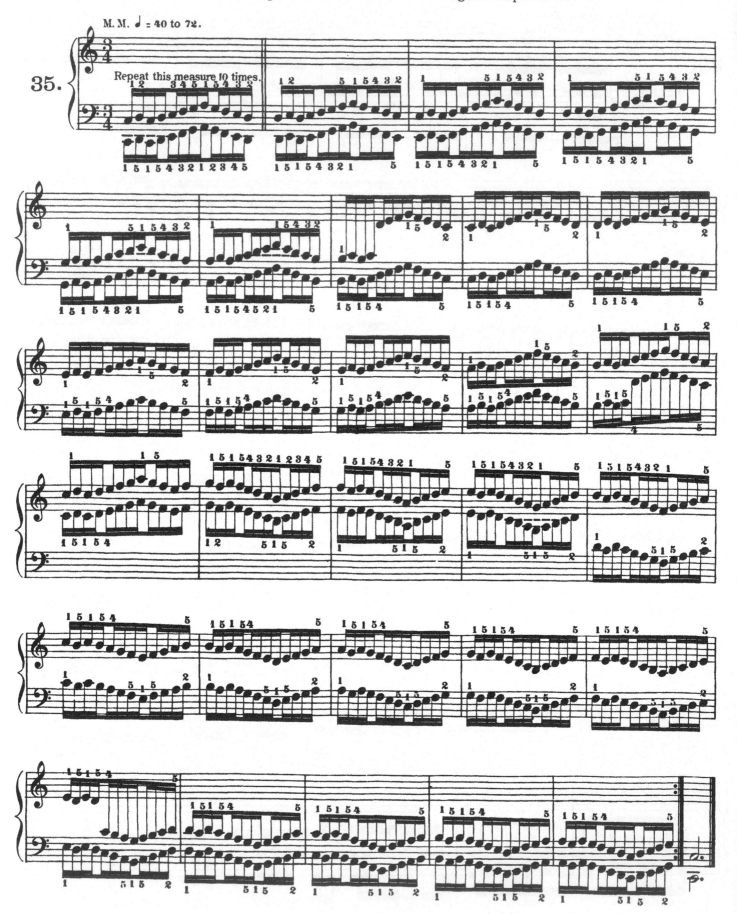

Another example of turning the thumb under.

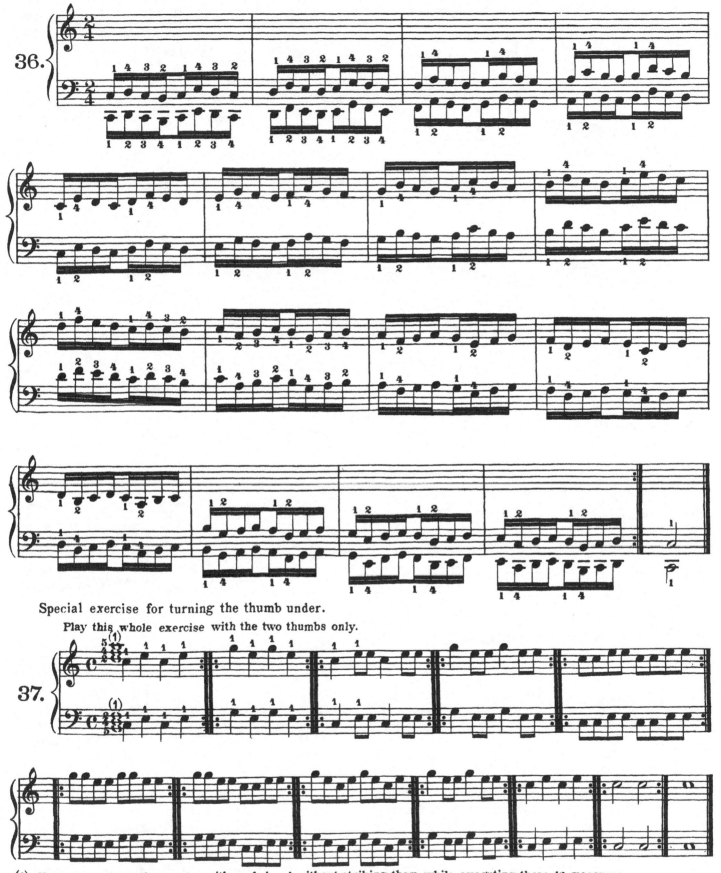

Special exercise for turning the thumb under.

Play this whole exercise with the two thumbs only.

(1) Hold down these three notes with each hand without striking them, while executing these 12 measures.

48

Preparatory exercise for the study of scales.

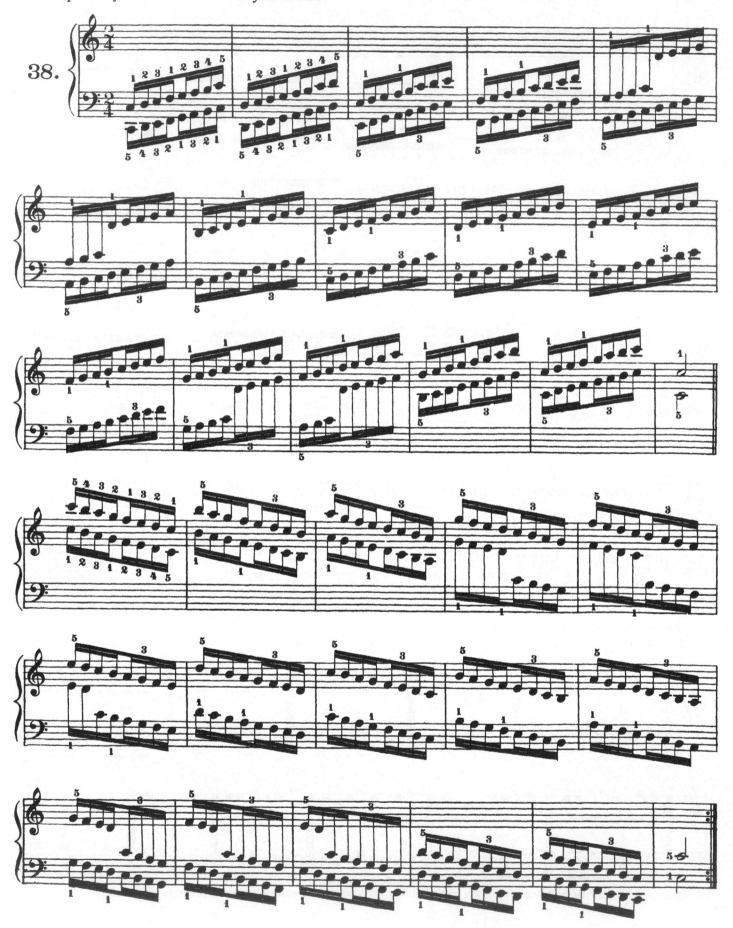

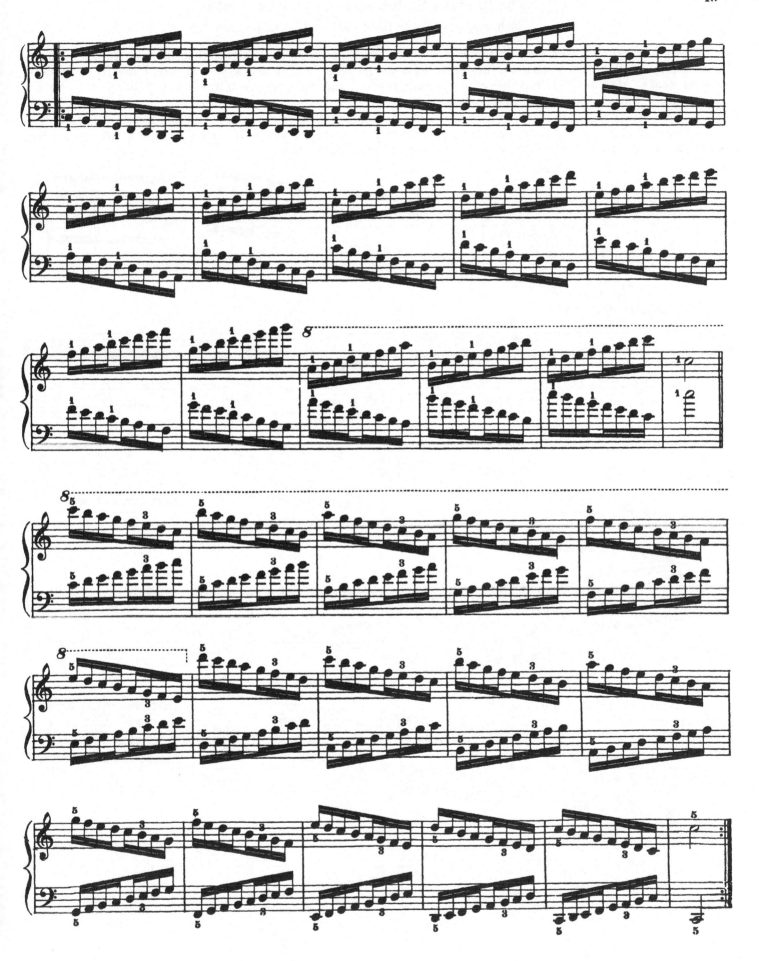

The 12 Major Scales, and the 12 Minor Scales.

Each major scale is followed by its relative minor.

There are two ways of playing the minor scale; we thought it best to give them here after each major scale, leaving it to the instructor to teach them as he sees fit. We mark by a figure 1 the first (modern) minor scale, also termed the "harmonic minor scale;" and by a figure 2 the second (ancient) minor scale, also termed the "melodic minor scale."

We know, that the modern or harmonic minor scale has a minor sixth and the leading-note both ascending and descending; whereas the ancient or melodic minor scale has a major sixth and the leading note is ascending, and a minor seventh and minor sixth in descending.

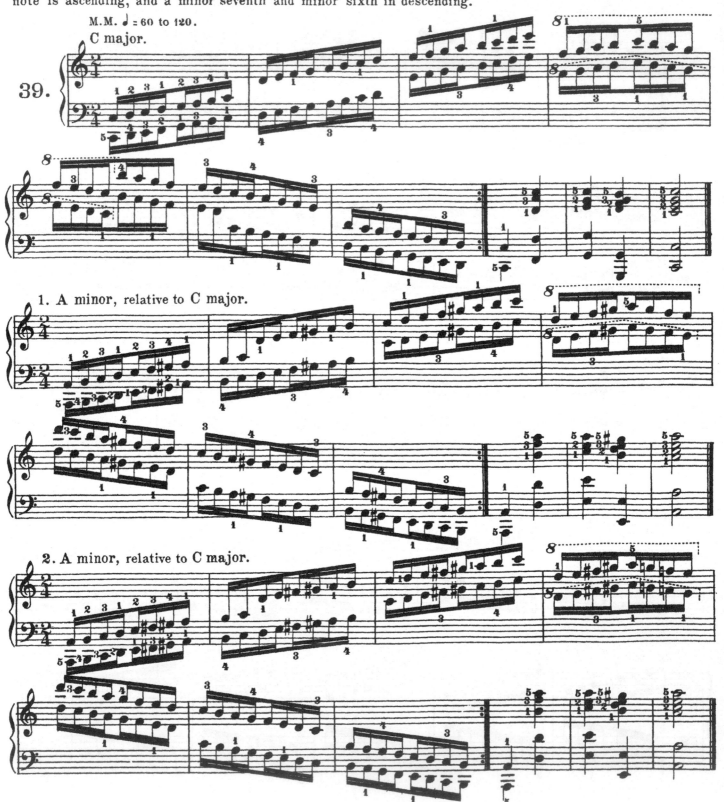

M.M. ♩ = 60 to 120.

C major.

39.

1. A minor, relative to C major.

2. A minor, relative to C major.

52

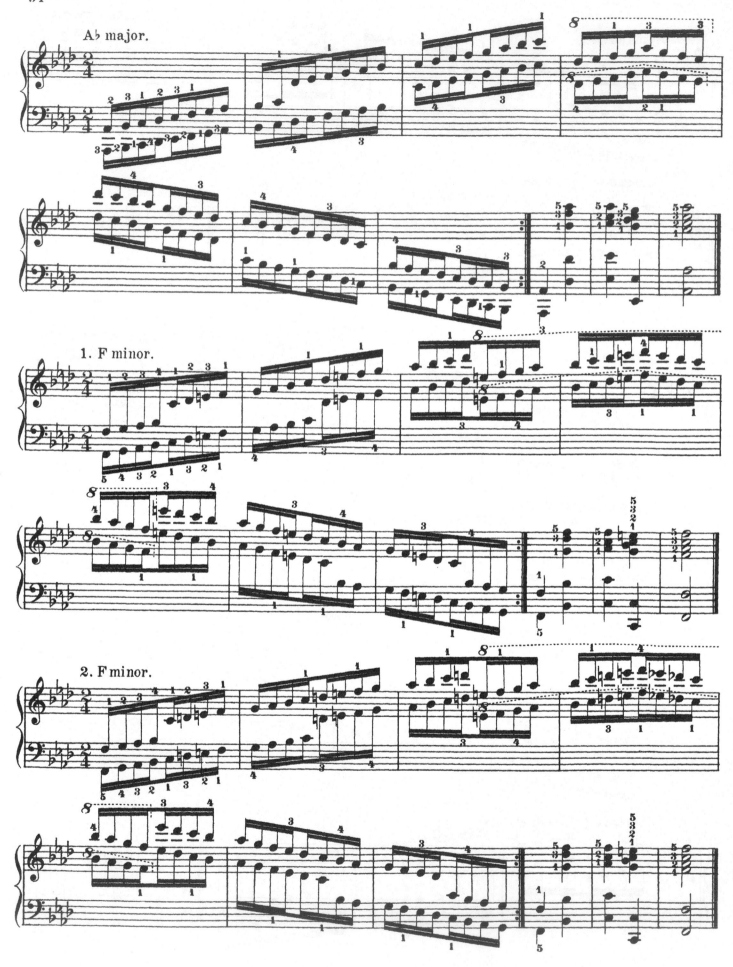

Ab major.

1. F minor.

2. F minor.

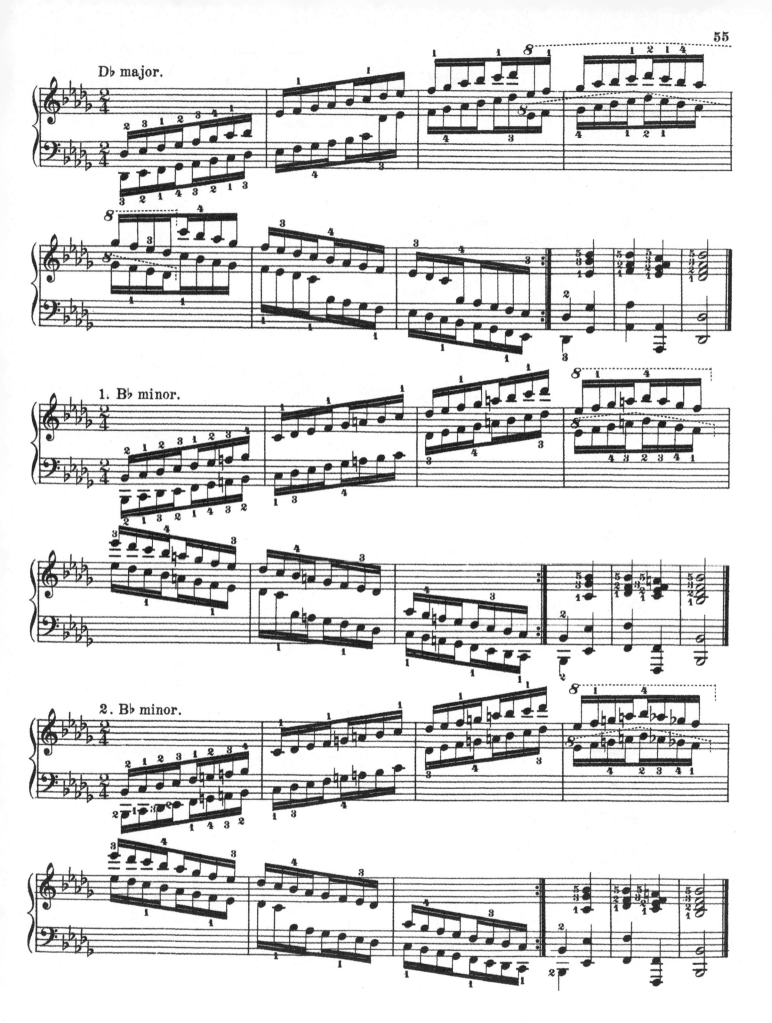

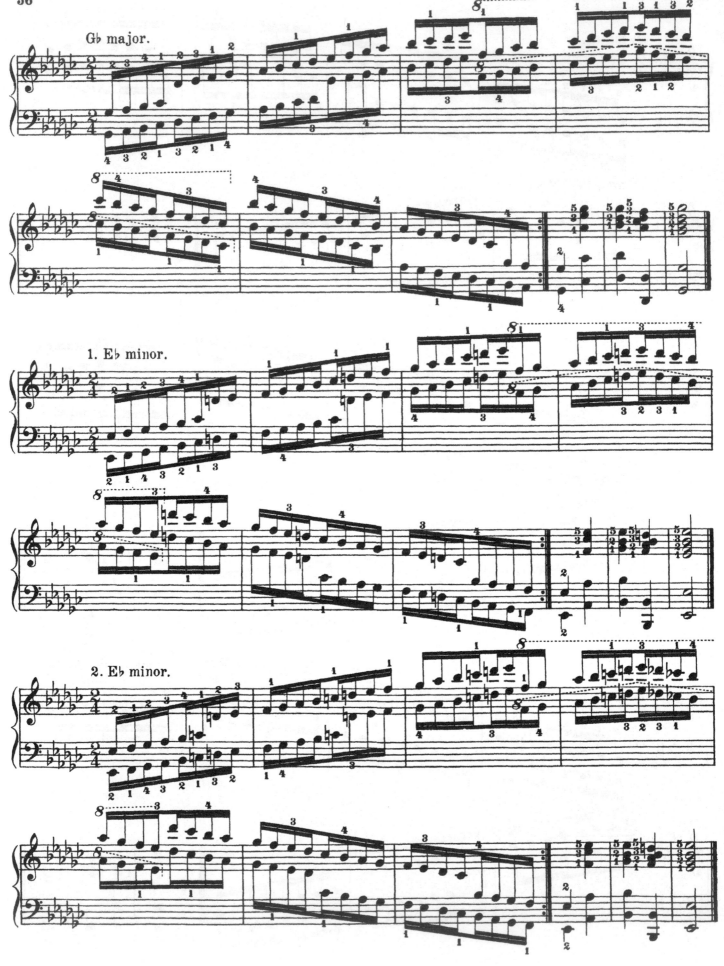

Gb major.

1. Eb minor.

2. Eb minor.

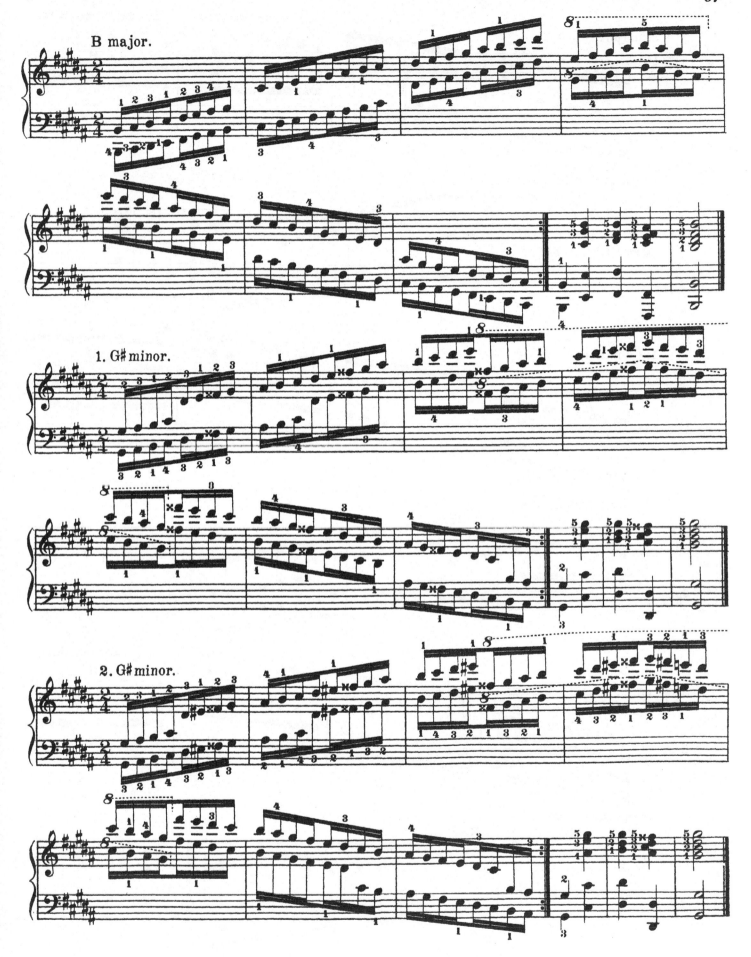

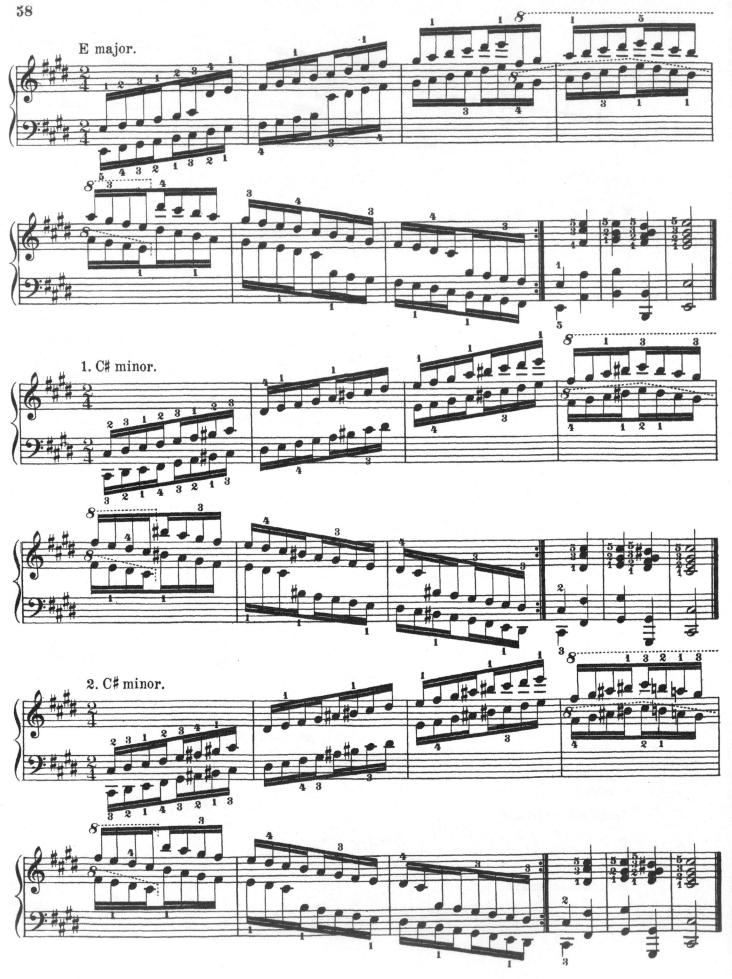

59

61

Chromatic Scales.

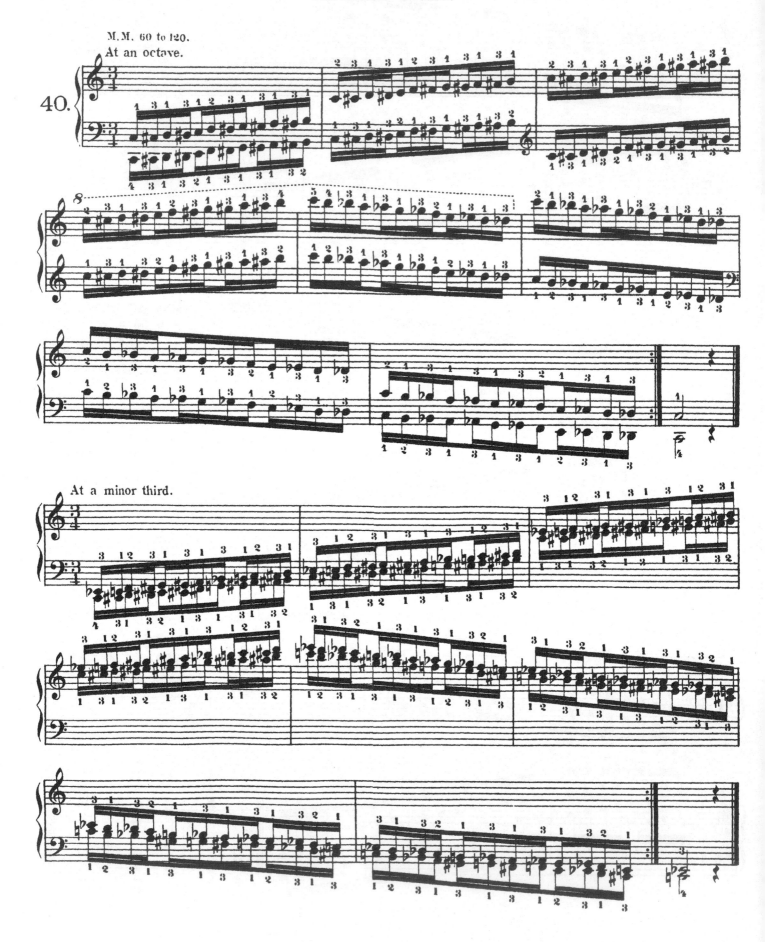

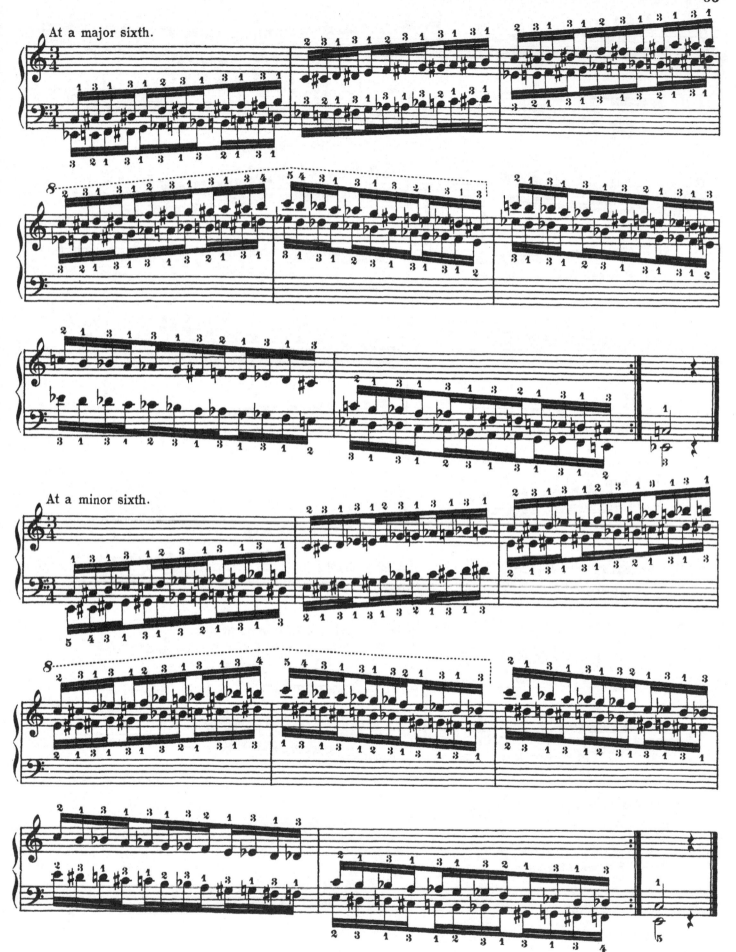

64 In contrary motion, beginning on the octave.

In contrary motion, beginning on the minor third.

In contrary motion, beginning on the major third.

Another fingering, which we particularly recommend for legato passages.

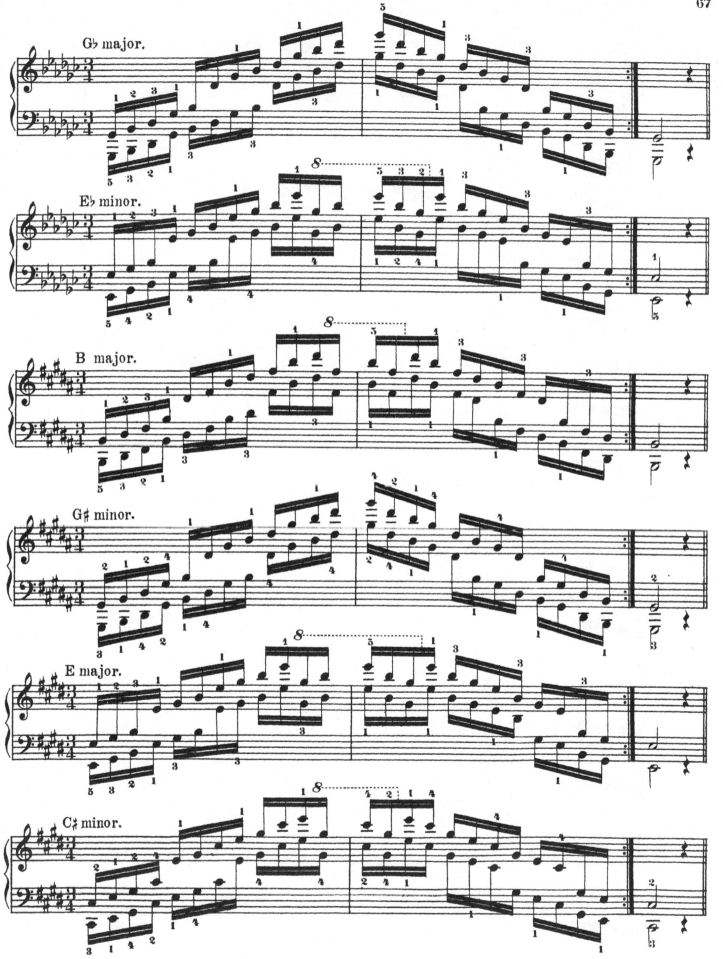

68

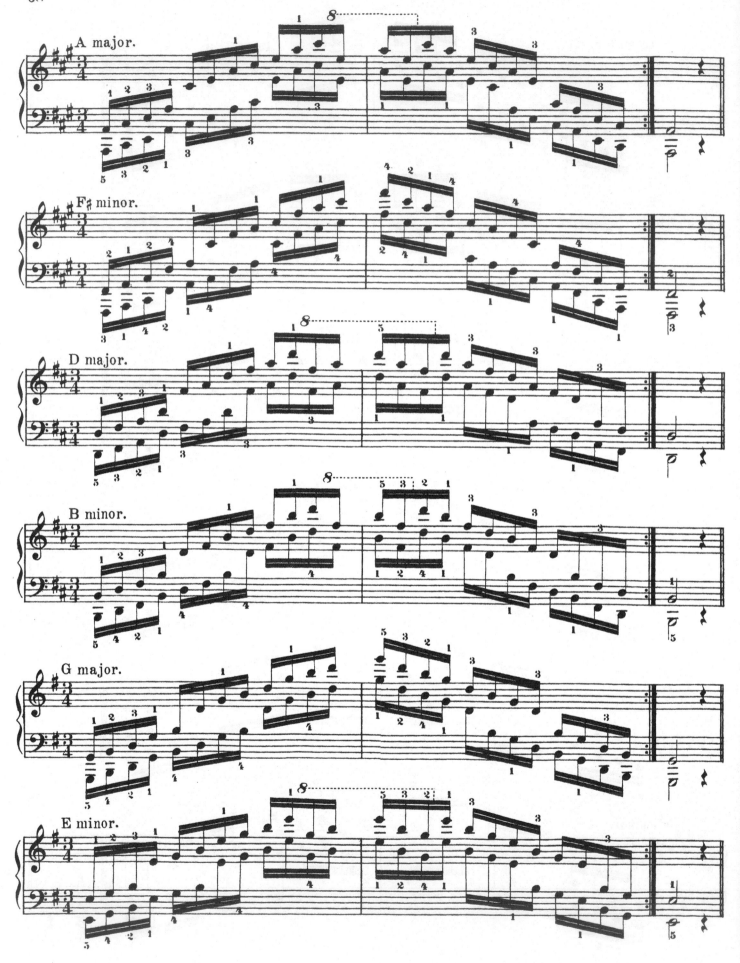

Extension (stretching) of the fingers
in chords of the diminished seventh, in arpeggios.

70

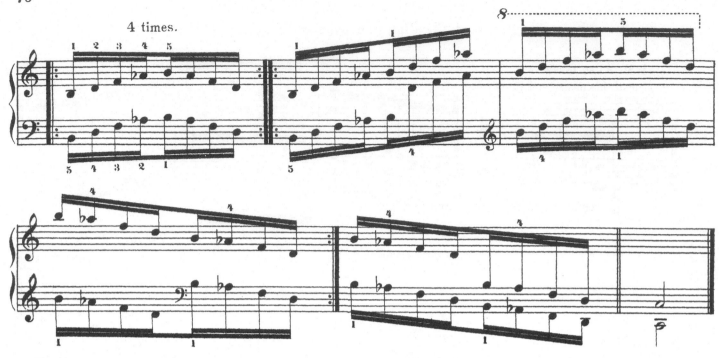

Extension of the fingers in chords of the dominant seventh, in arpeggios.

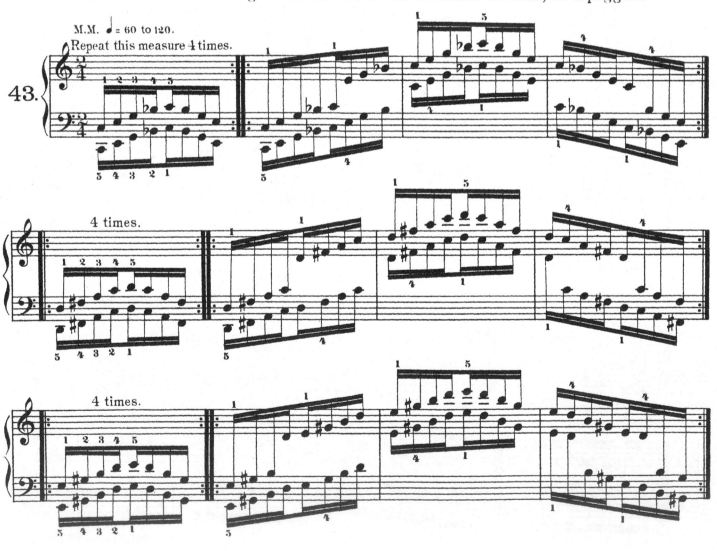

End of Part II.

Parts I and II of this work being the key to the difficulties in Part III, it is evidently very important that they should be thoroughly mastered before commencing the virtuoso studies contained in Part III.

The Virtuoso-Pianist. Part III

Virtuoso Exercises, for Obtaining a Mastery over the Greatest Mechanical Difficulties.

Notes repeated in groups of three.

Lift the fingers high and with precision, without raising hand or wrist. As soon as the first four measures are well learned, take up the rest of the exercise.

C. L. HANON

74

Notes repeated in groups of two, by all five fingers.

Study the first fingering until it is thoroughly mastered; practise similarly each of the five following fingerings then play through the whole exercise without stopping.

Accent the first of each pair of slurred notes.

(M.M. ♩ = 60 to 108)

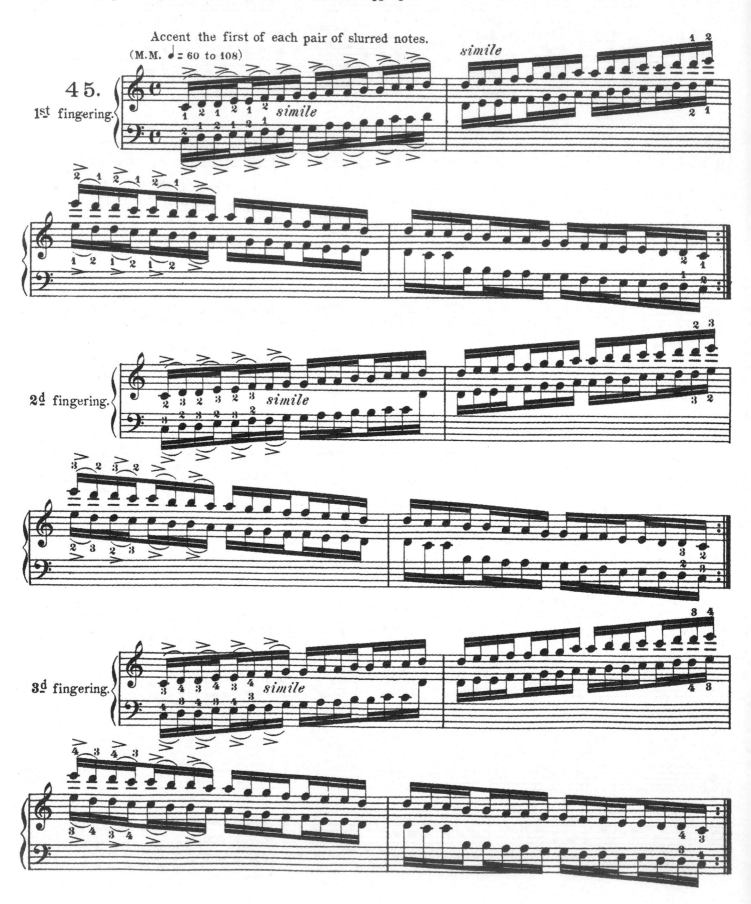

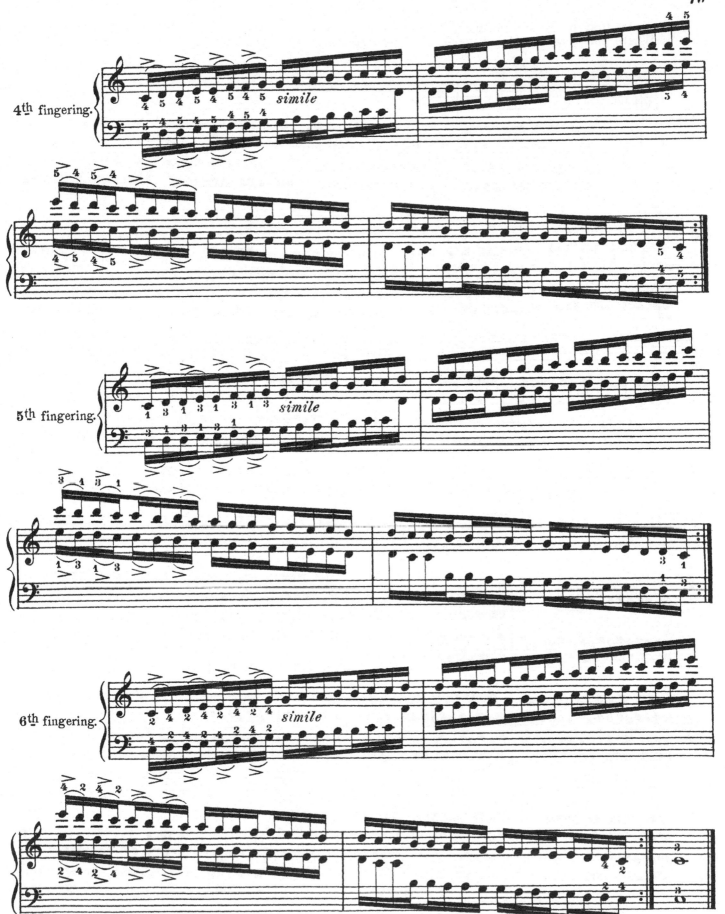

The Trill
for all five fingers.

Practise the first 6 measures until they can be executed in quite a rapid tempo; then practise the rest of the trill. Where the fingering is changed (1), be careful that not the slightest unevenness is apparent.

It is of interest to note that Mozart used this exercise for the study of the trill.

Thalberg's trill.

Notes repeated in groups of four.

Lift the fingers high and with precision throughout this exercise, without raising hand or wrist. When the first line is mastered, and not before, take up the rest of the exercise.

Wrist - exercise.
Detached Thirds and Sixths.

Lift the wrists well after each stroke, holding the arms perfectly quiet; the wrist should be supple, and the fingers firm without stiffness. Practise the first four measures until an easy wrist-movement is obtained; then take up the rest of the exercise.

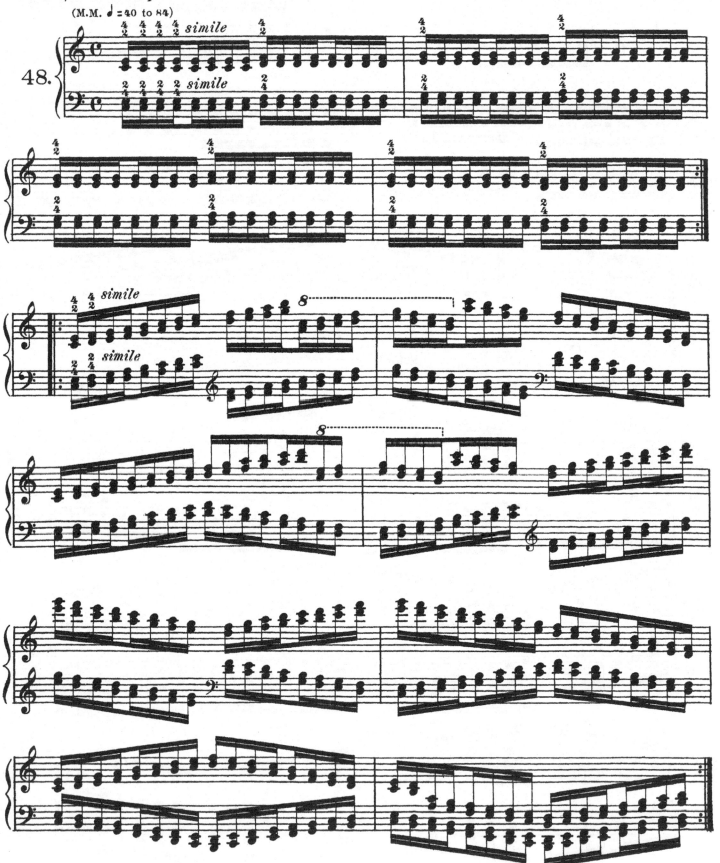

Detached Sixths.

Same remarks as for the thirds.
(M.M. ♩ = 40 to 84)

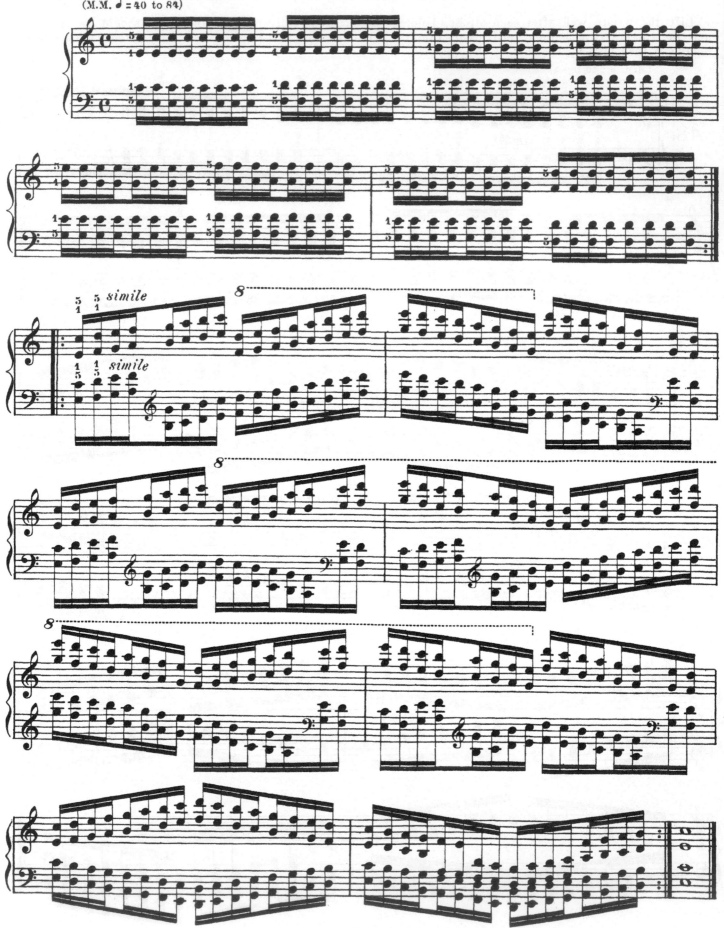

Stretches from the 1st to the 4th fingers, and from the 2d to the 5th, in each hand.

Very useful for increasing the stretching-capacity of these fingers.

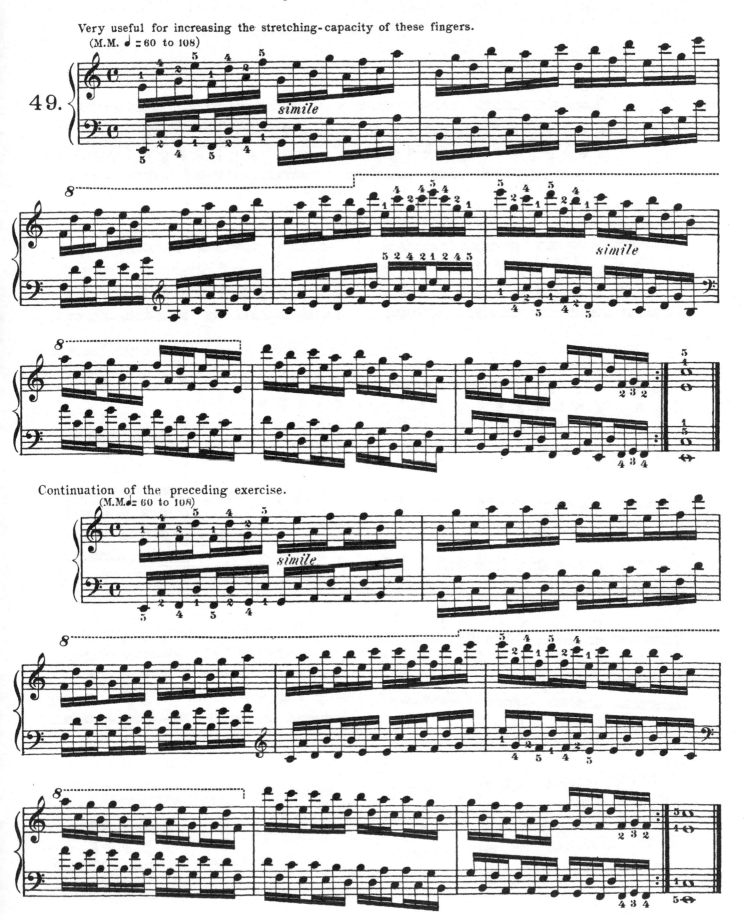

Continuation of the preceding exercise.

Legato Thirds.

We recommend careful study of this exercise, as Thirds occupy a very important place in difficult music. All notes must be struck evenly and very distinctly.

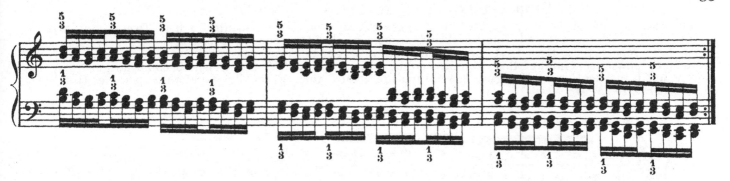

Scales in Legato Thirds. It is indispensable to practise scales in legato thirds. To obtain a smooth legato, keep the fifth finger of the right hand for an instant on its note while the thumb and 3d finger are passing over to the next third; in the left hand, the thumb is similarly held for an instant. Notes to be held are indicated by half-notes.(1) Proceed similarly in the chrormatic scale further on, and in all scales in Thirds.

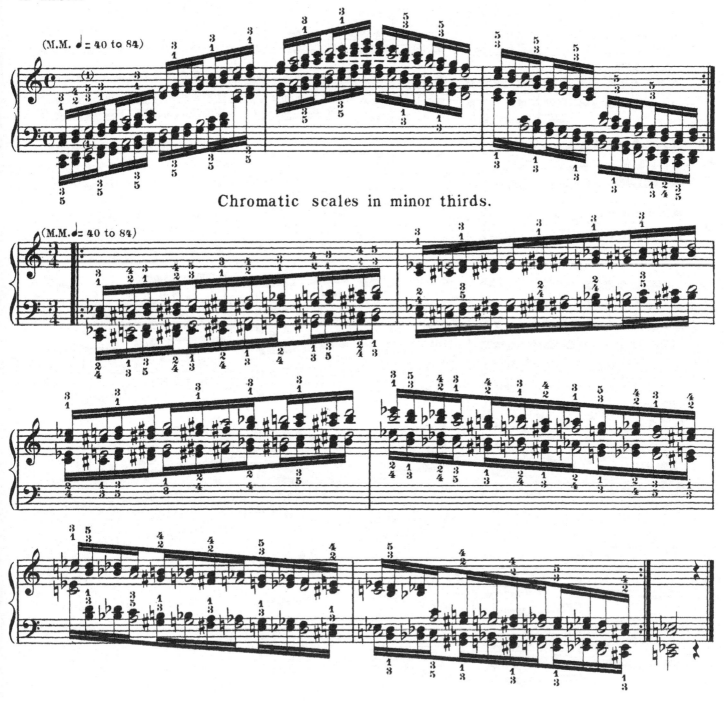

Chromatic scales in minor thirds.

Preparatory Exercise for Scales in Octaves.

The wrists should be very supple, the fingers taking the octaves should be held firmly but without stiffness, and the unoccupied fingers should assume a slightly rounded position.

At first repeat these three first lines slowly until a good wrist-movement is attained, and then accelerate the tempo, continuing the exercise without interruption. If the wrists become fatigued, play more slowly until the feeling of fatigue has disappeared, and then gradually accelerate up to the first tempo. *See remarks to Nº 48.*

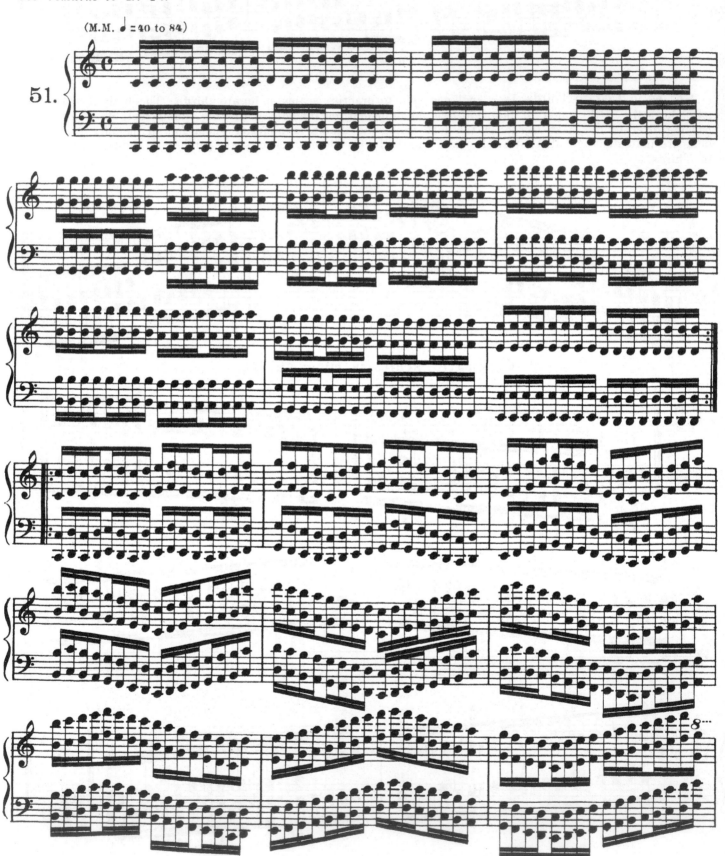

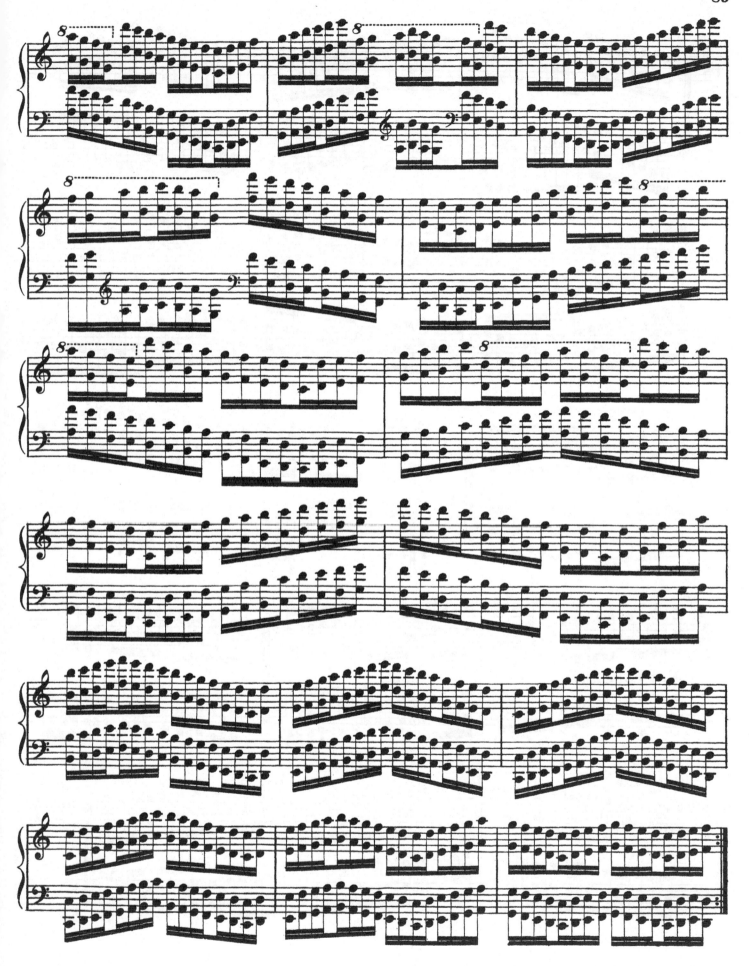

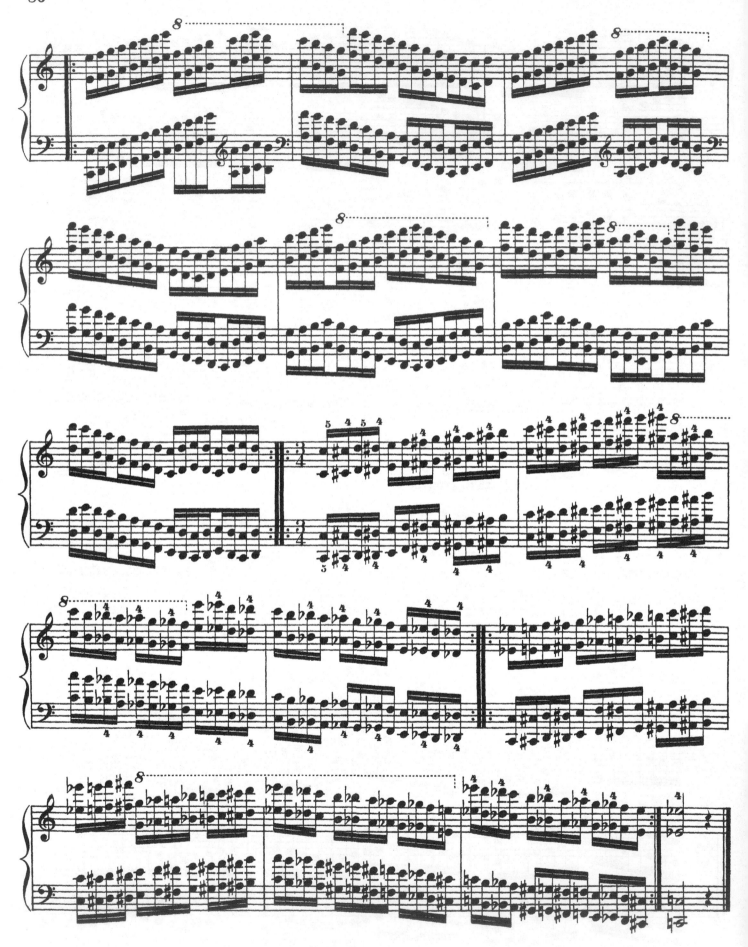

Play these scales legato, and very evenly; it is highly important to master them thoroughly. *See* remarks to № 50.

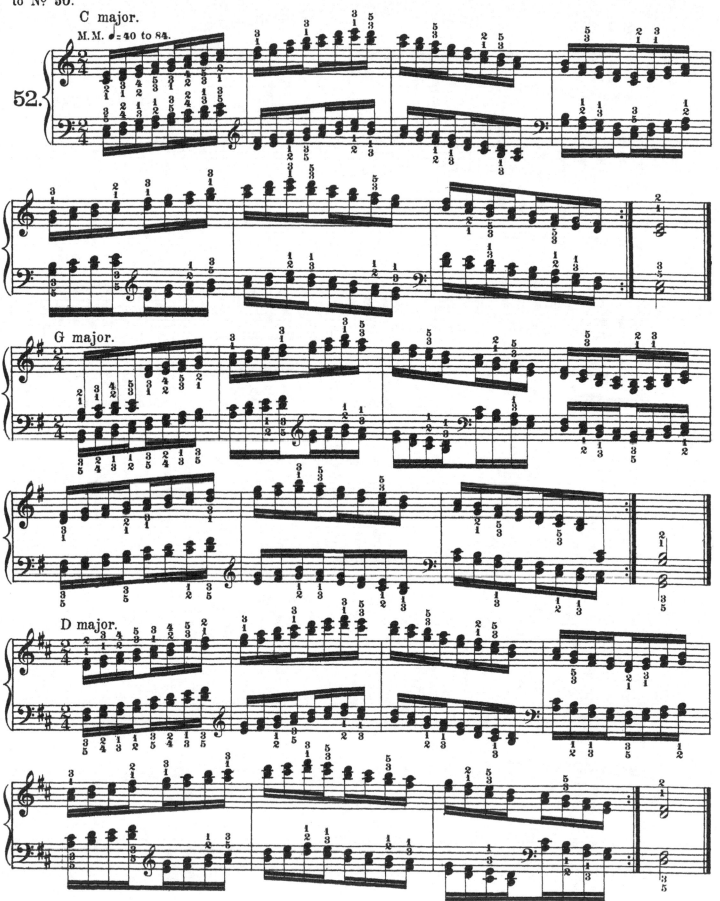

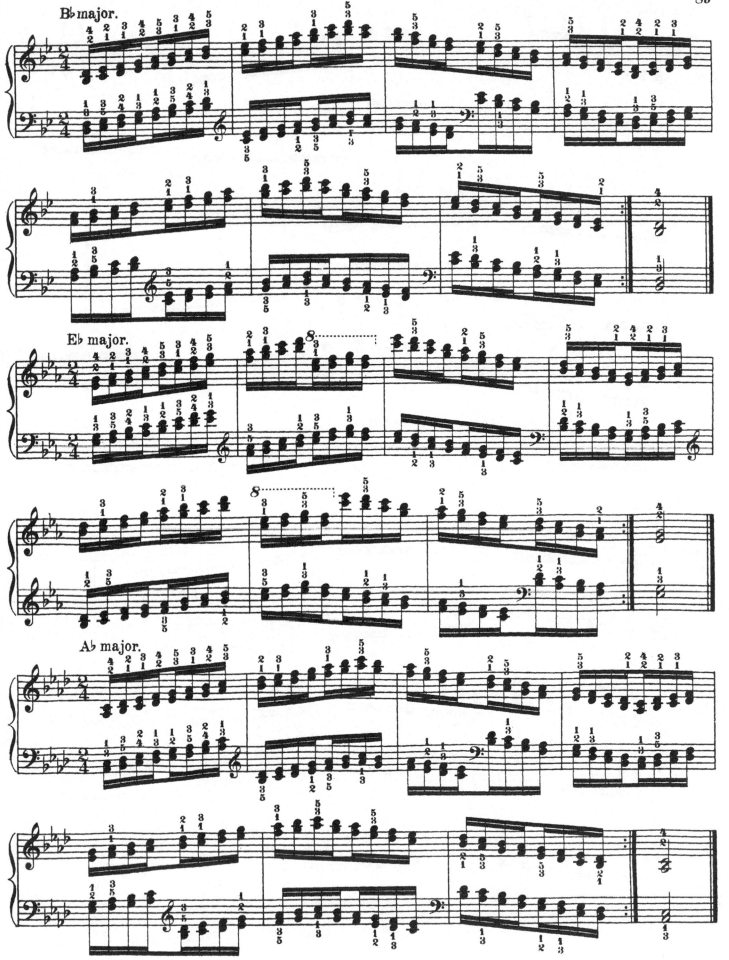

First practise each of these scales until it can be executed with facility; then play through all 24 without interruption.

We cannot too strongly insist on the absolute necessity of a proper wrist-movement; it is the only means of executing octaves without stiffness, and with suppleness, vivacity and energy.

See the explanations for Nos 48 and 51.

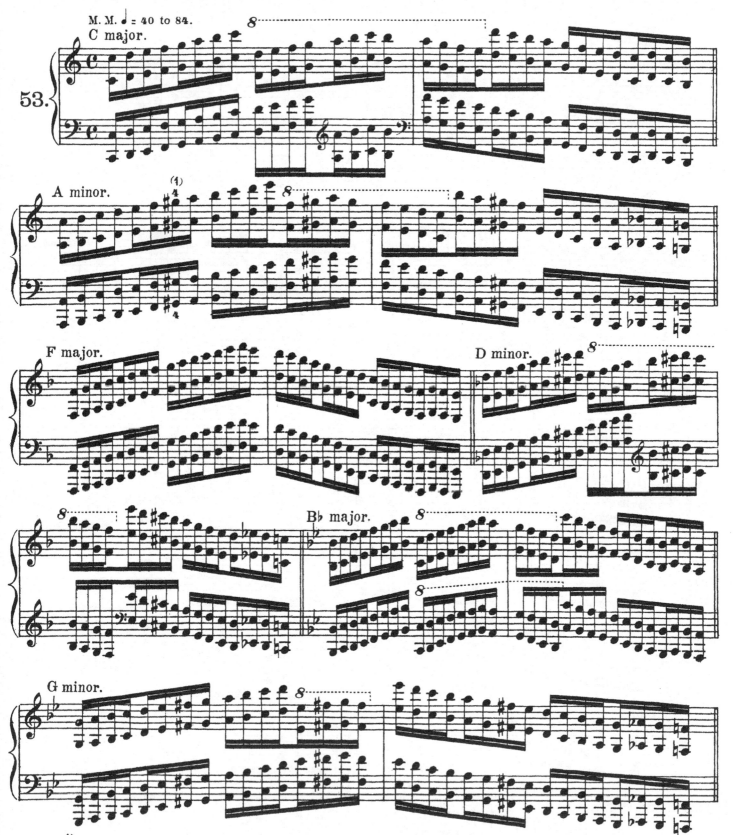

(1) In all scales in Octaves, the black keys are to be taken with the 4th finger of either hand.

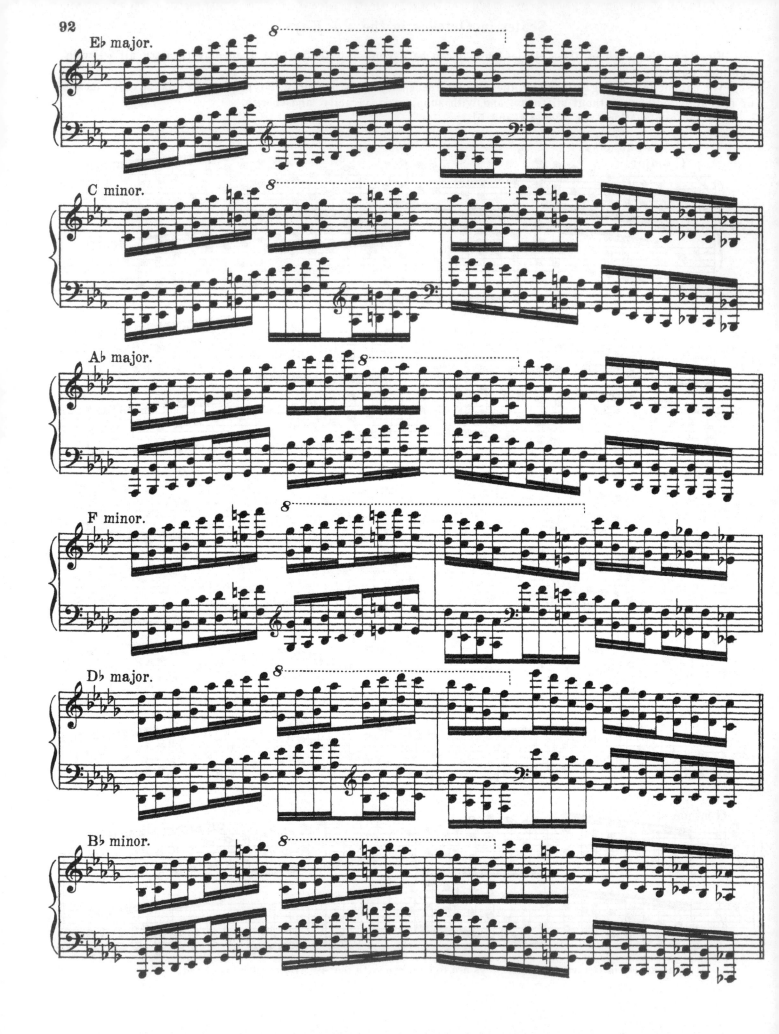

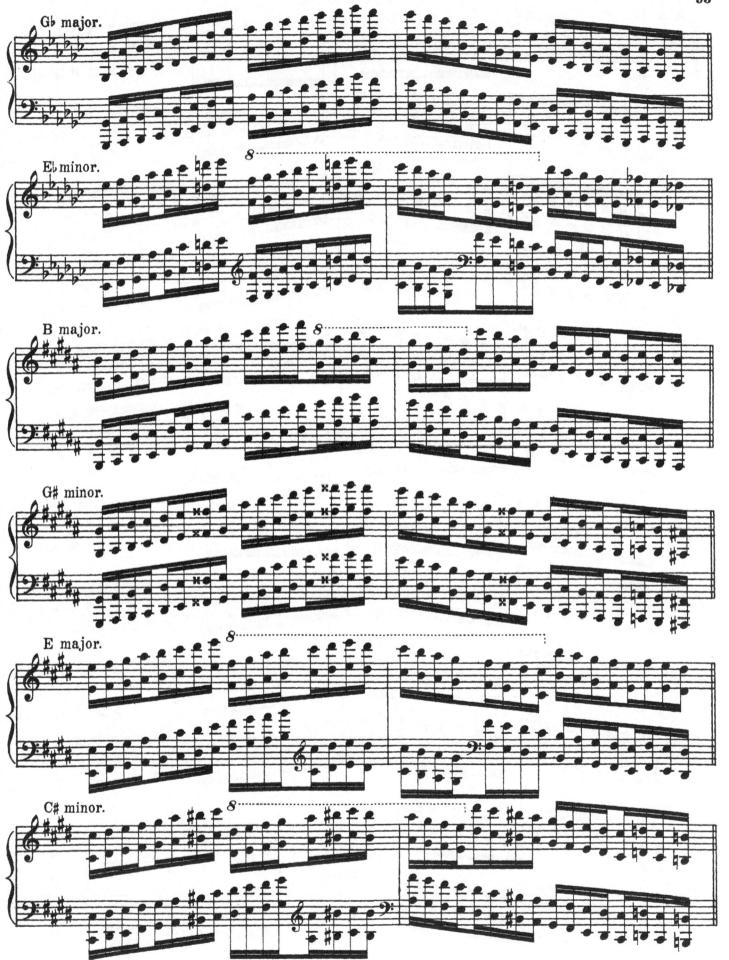

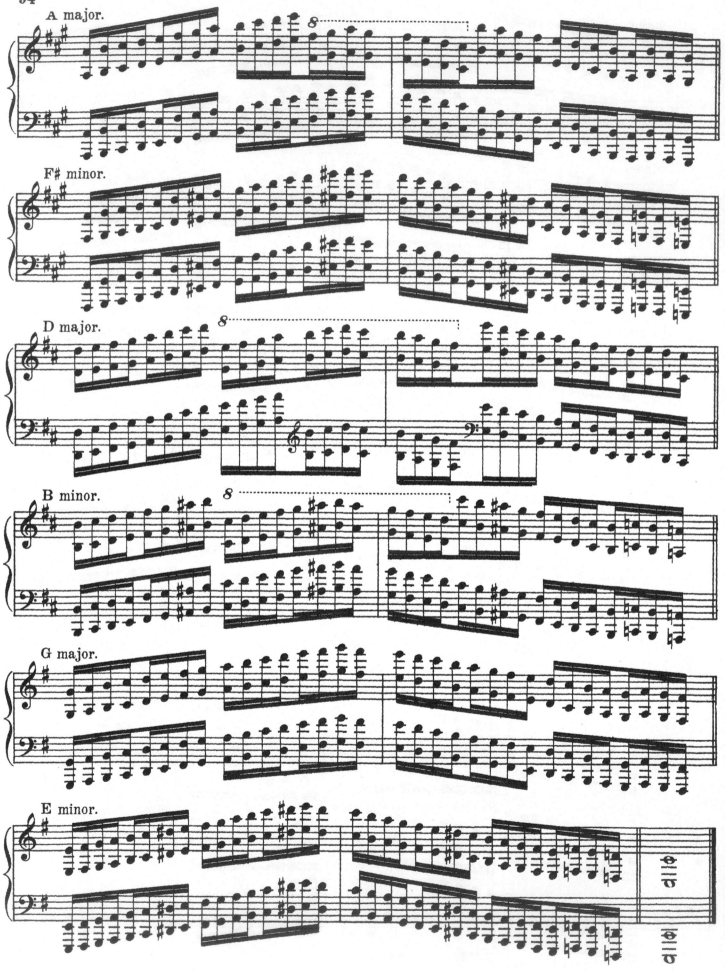

The Fourfold Trill in Thirds, for all five fingers.

Execute this exercise very smoothly and evenly, striking each Third very clearly.

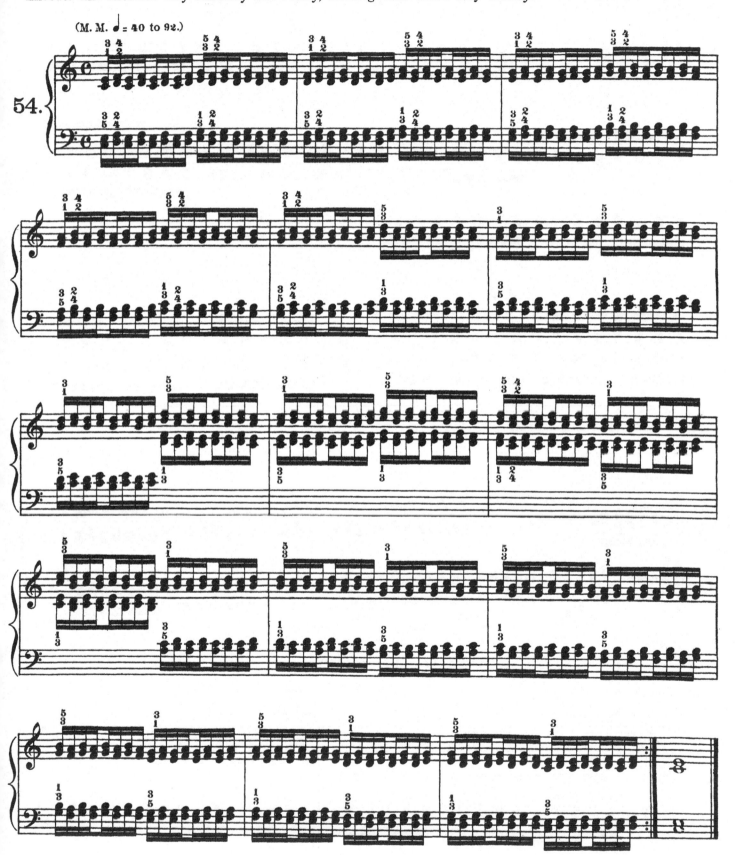

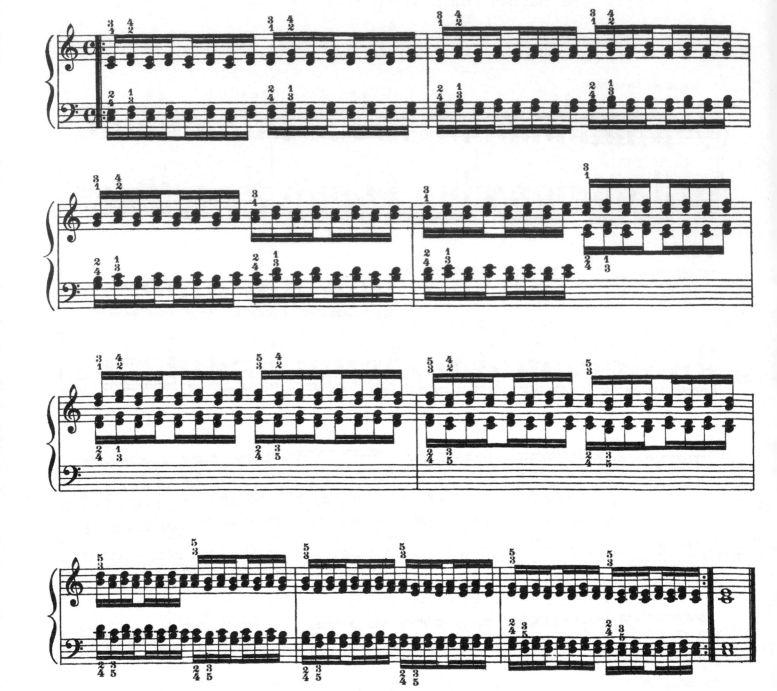

The Threefold Trill.

Same remark as for № 54.

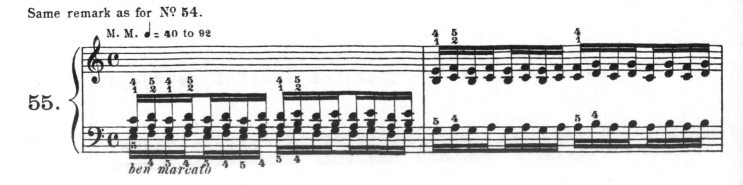

M. M. ♩ = 40 to 92

55.

ben marcato

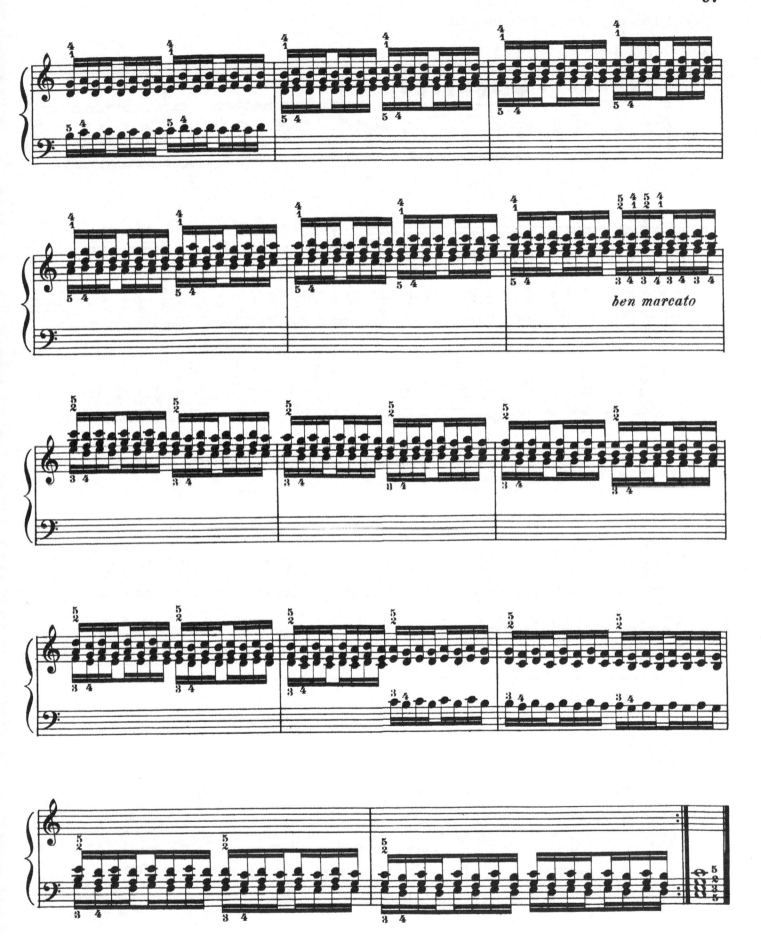

Special fingerings for the fourfold Trill.

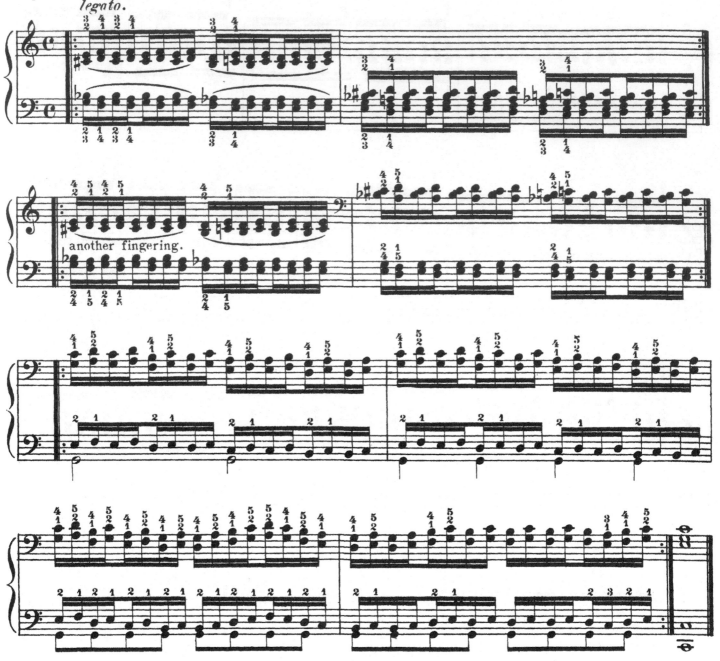

Scales in Broken Octaves, in the 24 Keys.

Play them through without stopping.
This highly important exercise likewise prepares the wrists for the study of the tremolo.

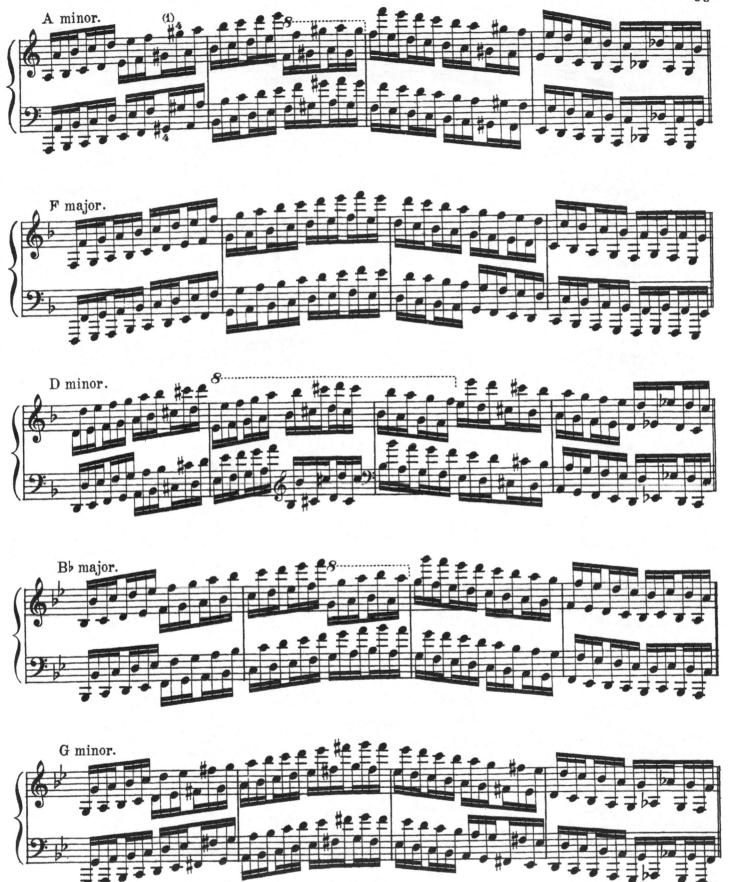

(1) Thoughout this exercise, take the black keys with the 4th finger of each hand.

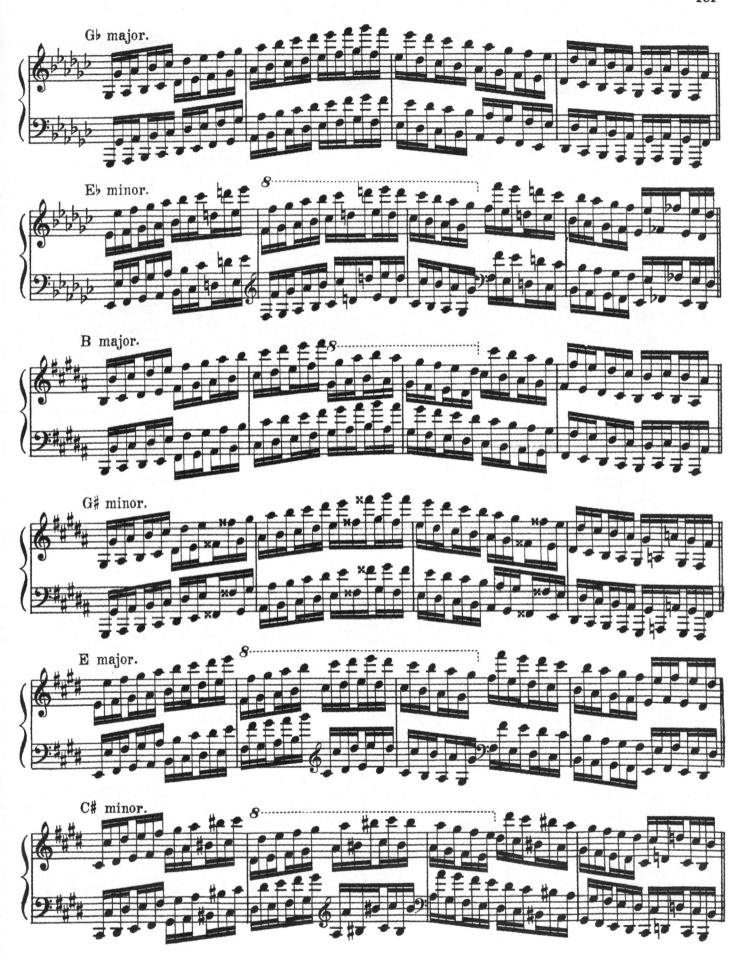

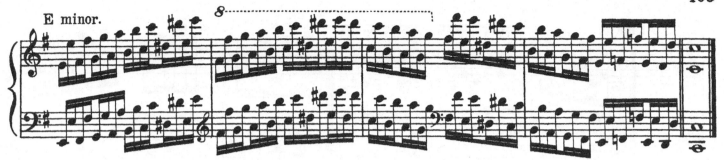

Broken Arpeggios in Octaves, in the 24 Keys.

To begin with, practise the first arpeggio in C. which must be played cleanly and distinctly, with a good wrist-movement, before passing to the next in minor.

Similarly practise each of the 24 arpeggios; then play them all through without interruption.

M. M. ♩ = 40 to 72

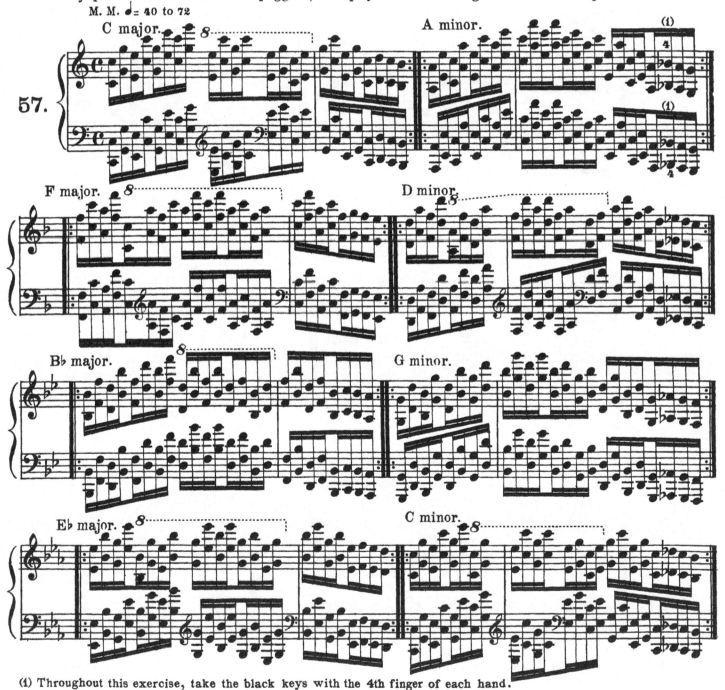

(1) Throughout this exercise, take the black keys with the 4th finger of each hand.

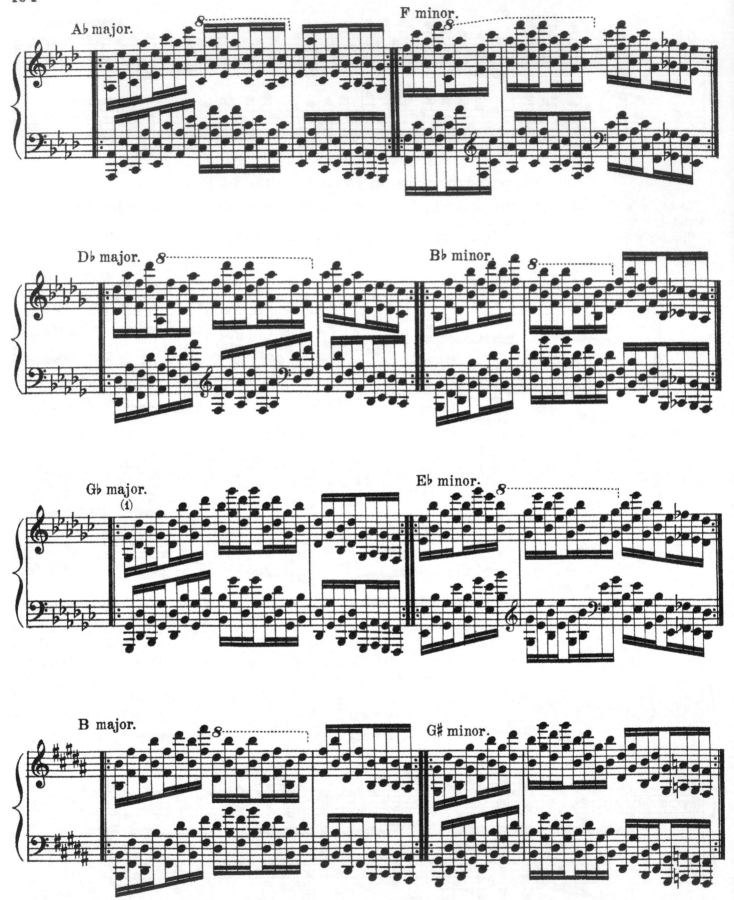

(1) As this arpeggio, and the next one in E♭ minor, are on black keys alone, it makes no difference whether the 4th or 5th finger be employed.

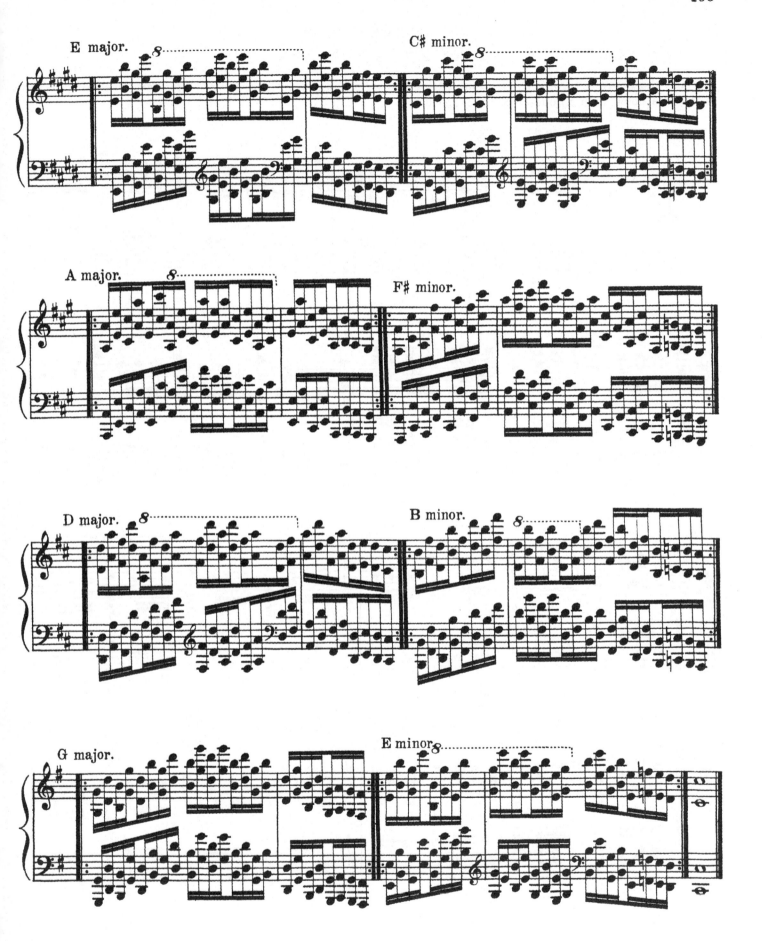

Sustained Octaves.
accompanied by detached notes.

Strike the octaves vigorously without lifting the wrists, and hold them down while deftly executing the intermediate notes with a good finger-movement

Fourfold Trill in Sixths,

for the combination of the 1st and 4th, and 2nd and 5th, fingers of each hand.

Neither hand nor wrist should be moved in the least while playing this exercise.

(M. M. ♩ = 40 to 84)

59.

Repeat this measure 4 times.

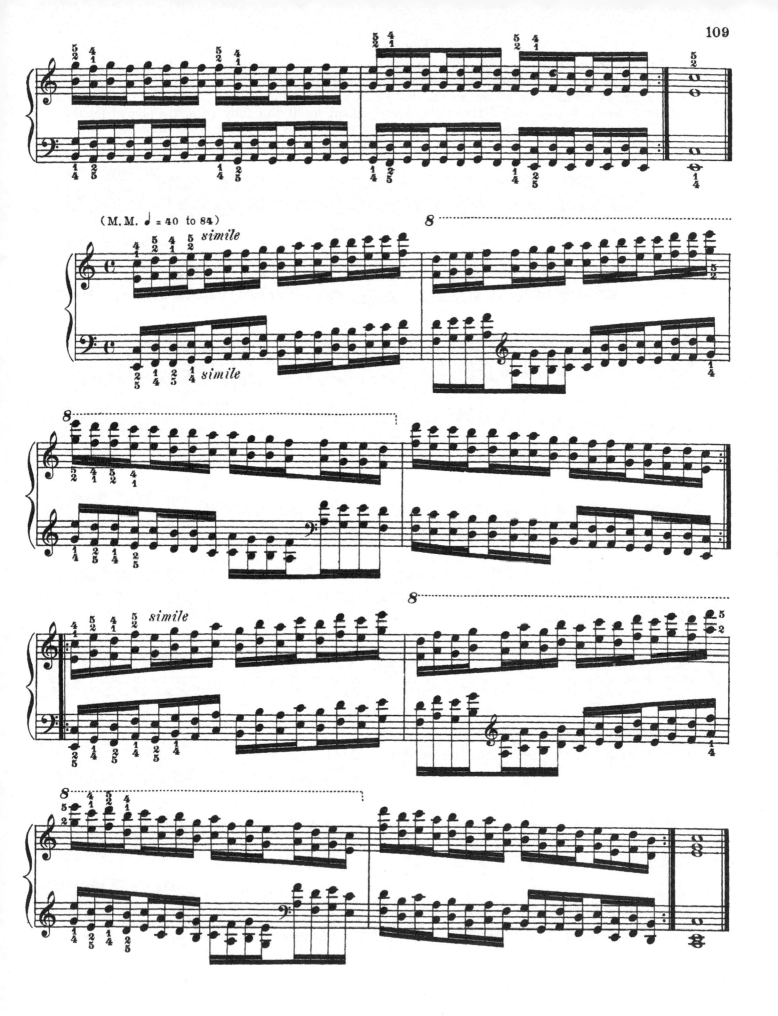

The Tremolo.

To properly execute the tremolo, it should be played with the same rapidity as the roll on the drum.

Practise slowly at first; then gradually accelerate the tempo until the movement indicated (M.M. ♩=72) is reached. Finally, by oscillations of the wrists, the rapidity is still further augmented up to the tempo of the drum-roll. This etude is long and difficult; but the excellent result will fully repay the pianist for the trouble and fatigue encountered. Steibelt made his hearers shiver by his execution of the tremolo.

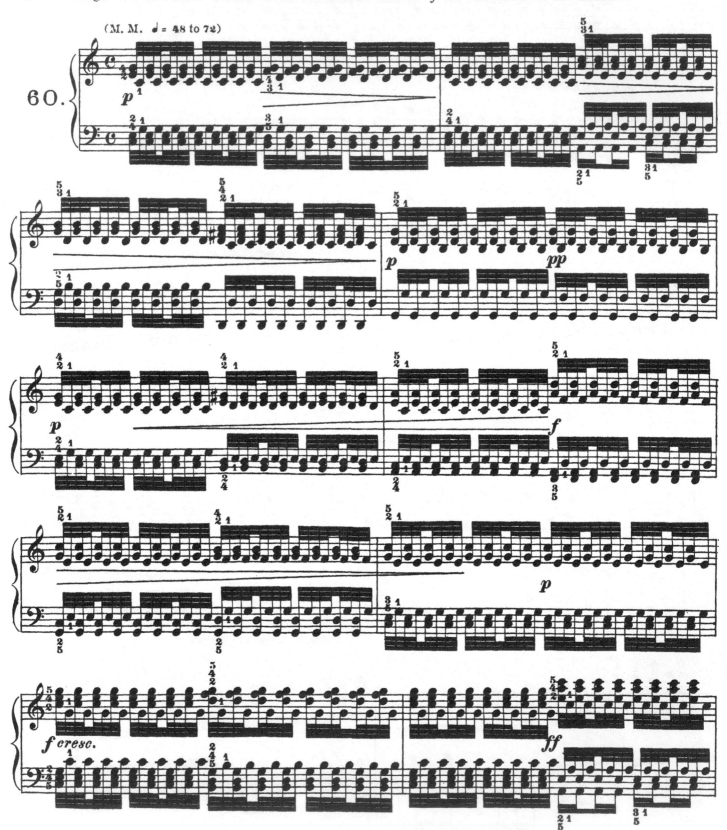

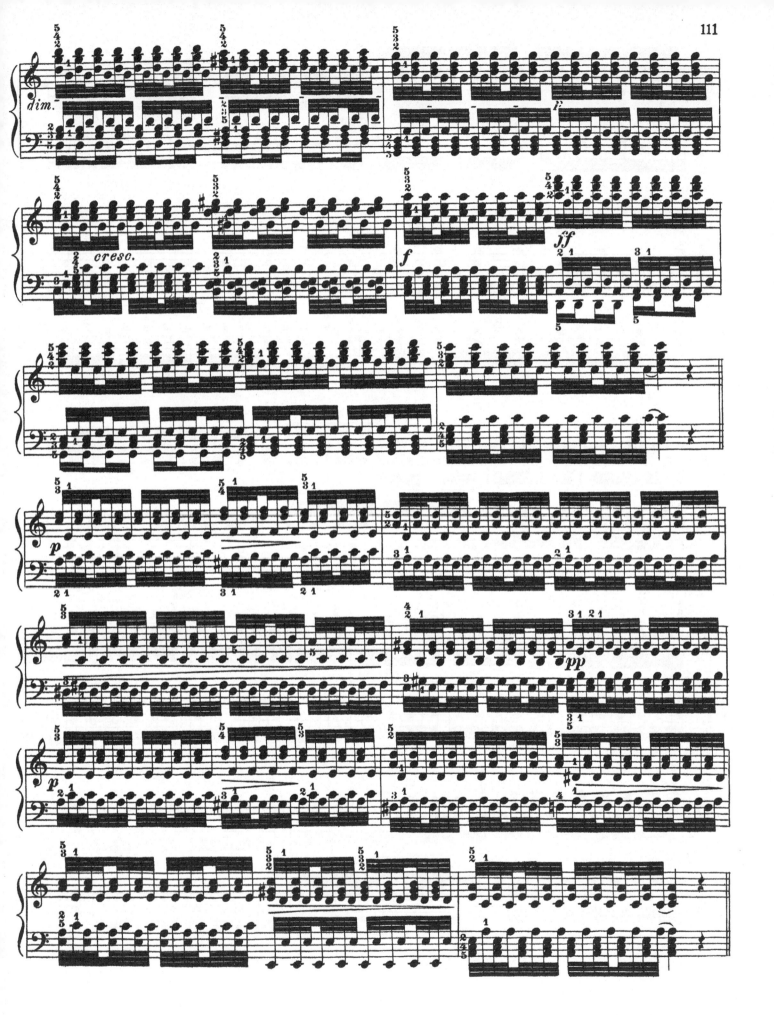

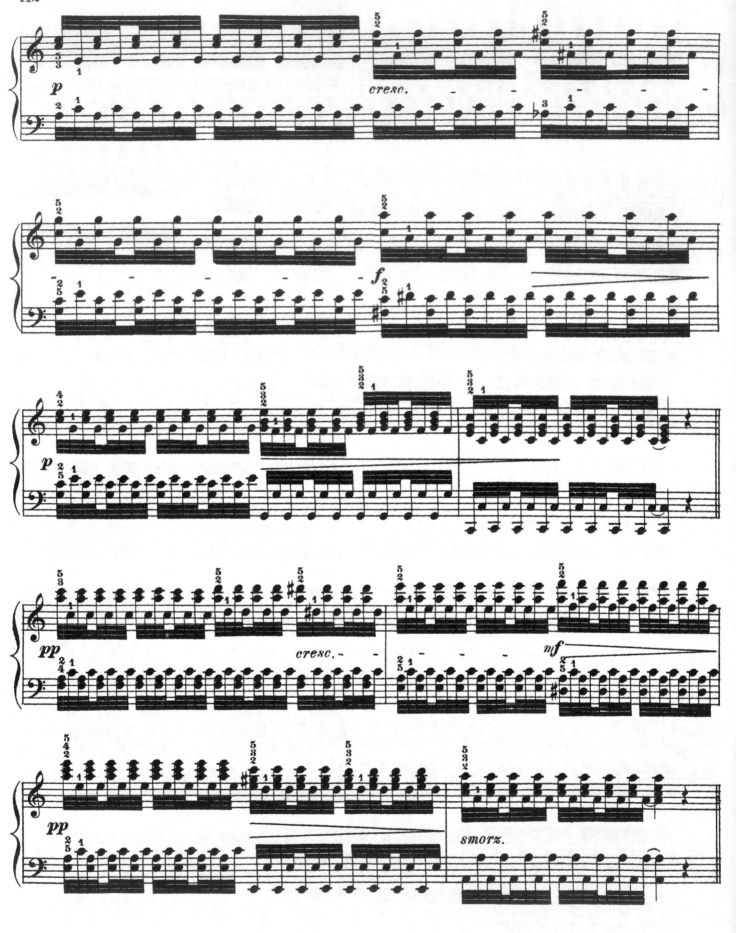

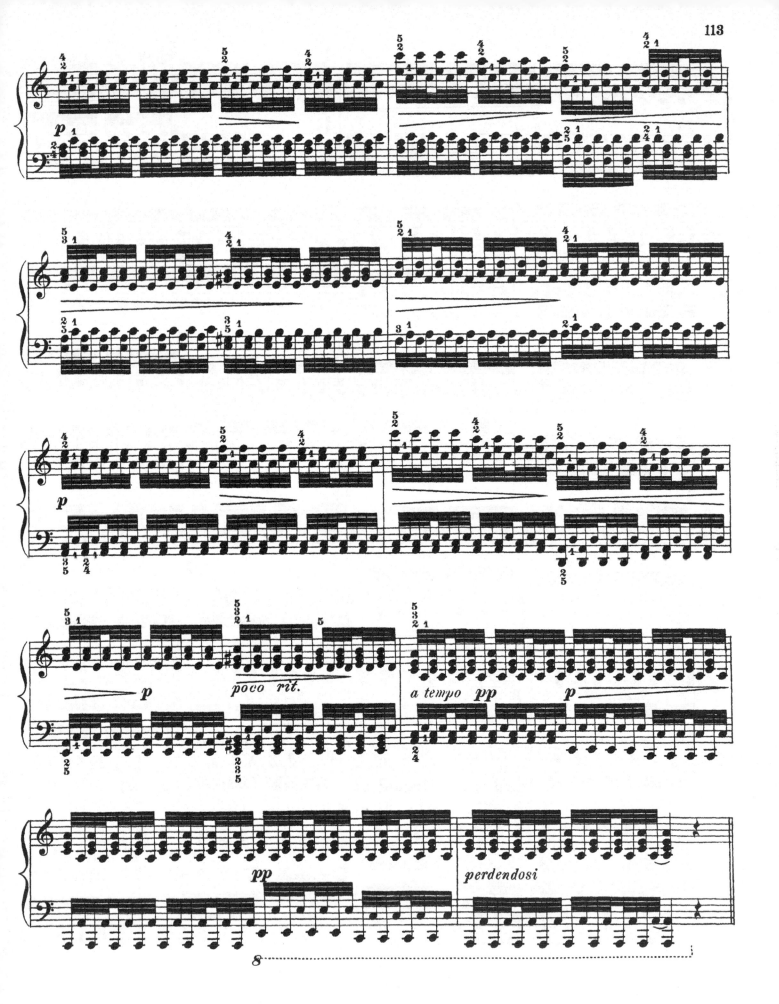

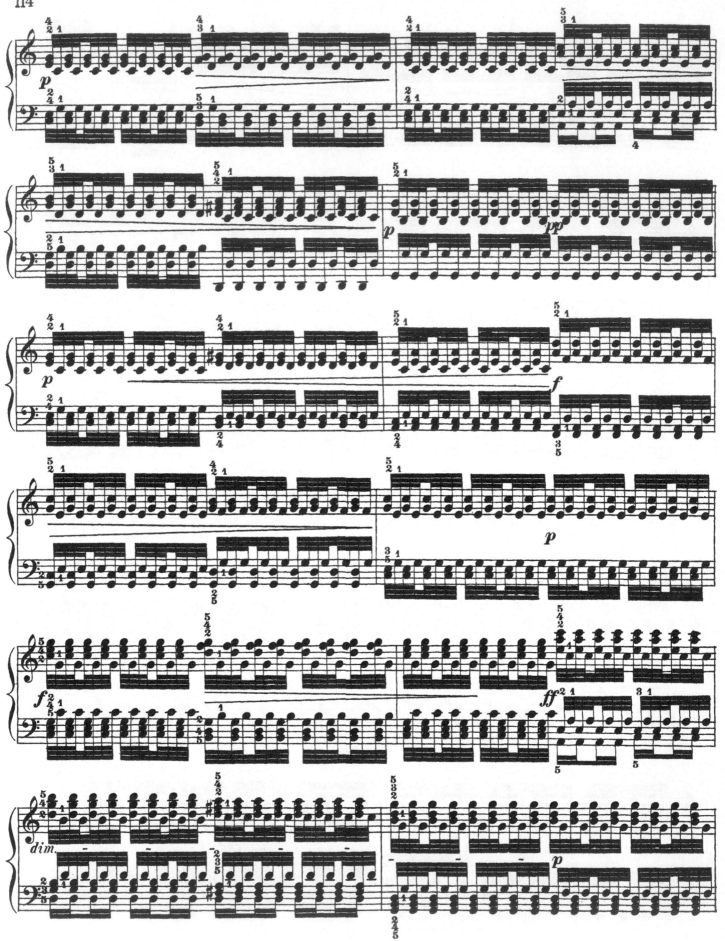

Concluding Remarks.

Now that the student has practised this entire volume, he is acquainted with the chief mechanical difficulties; but, if he would enjoy the fruit of his toil, and become a real virtuoso, he ought to play this entire book through every day for a certain time; only in this way can he familiarize himself with these great difficulties. An hour is required to play the book through.

The greatest artists find it necessary to repeat daily exercises for several hours, merely to "keep up their playing." We should not, therefore, be accused of exaggerating the matter when we require of a student aspiring to true virtuosity, that he should play these exercises through every day.

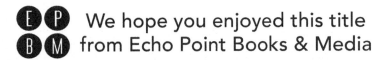 We hope you enjoyed this title
from Echo Point Books & Media

Before Closing this Book, Two Good Things to Know

Buy Direct & Save

Go to www.echopointbooks.com (click "Our Titles" at top or click "For Echo Point Publishing" in the middle) to see our complete list of titles. We publish books on a wide variety of topics—from spirituality to auto repair.

Buy direct and save 10% at www.echopointbooks.com

DISCOUNT CODE: EPBUYER

Make Literary History and Earn $100 Plus Other Goodies Simply for Your Book Recommendation!

At Echo Point Books & Media we specialize in republishing out-of-print books that are united by one essential ingredient: high quality. Do you know of any great books that are no longer actively published? If so, please let us know. If we end up publishing your recommendation, you'll be adding a wee bit to literary culture and a bunch to our publishing efforts.

Here is how we will thank you:

- A free copy of the new version of your beloved book that includes acknowledgement of your skill as a sharp book scout.

- A free copy of another Echo Point title you like from echopointbooks.com.

- And, oh yes, we'll also send you a check for $100.

Since we publish an eclectic list of titles, we're interested in a wide range of books. So please don't be shy if you have obscure tastes or like books with a practical focus. To get a sense of what kind of books we publish, visit us at www.echopointbooks.com.

If you have a book that you think will work for us,
send us an email at editorial@echopointbooks.com

  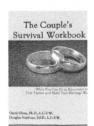  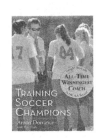

CPSIA information can be obtained
at www.ICGtesting.com
Printed in the USA
BVOW10*2349010917
493560BV00019B/321/P